D1562474

The Two-Headed Whale

Sandy Winterbottom

The
TWO-HEADED
WHALE

Life, Loss, and the
Tangled Legacy of Whaling
in the Antarctic

DAVID SUZUKI INSTITUTE

GREYSTONE BOOKS
Vancouver/Berkeley/London

First published in North America, Australia,
and New Zealand by Greystone Books in 2023
Originally published in the U.K. as *The Two-Headed Whale*,
copyright © 2022 by Sandy Winterbottom, by Birlinn Limited

23 24 25 26 27   5 4 3 2 1

Greystone Books Ltd.
greystonebooks.com

David Suzuki Institute
davidsuzukiinstitute.org

Cataloguing data available from Library and Archives Canada
978-1-77840-090-2 (cloth)
978-1-77840-091-9 (epub)

Proofreading by Tracy Bordian
Jacket design by Jessica Sullivan
Jacket illustration by iStock.com

Printed and bound in Canada on FSC® certified paper
at Friesens. The FSC® label means that materials used for
the product have been responsibly sourced.

Greystone Books thanks the Canada Council for the Arts, the
British Columbia Arts Council, the Province of British Columbia
through the Book Publishing Tax Credit, and the Government
of Canada for supporting our publishing activities.

Canada

MIX
Paper from
responsible sources
FSC
www.fsc.org   FSC® C016245

BRITISH
COLUMBIA

BRITISH COLUMBIA
ARTS COUNCIL
An agency of the Province of British Columbia

Canada Council   Conseil des arts
for the Arts   du Canada

Greystone Books gratefully acknowledges the xʷməθkʷəy̓əm (Musqueam),
Sḵwx̱wú7mesh (Squamish), and səlilwətaɬ (Tsleil-Waututh) peoples on
whose land our Vancouver head office is located.

For G

Contents

Forecast   *ix*

Part One: SOUTH

1   Orientation   *3*
2   Navigation   *27*
3   Landfall   *51*

Part Two: BLUE

4   Into the Blue   *79*
5   Antarctic Blue   *113*
6   El Fin del Mundo   *147*

Part Three: NORTH

7   Search Patterns   *179*
8   The Last Whalers   *197*
9   Out of the Blue   *209*

Outlook   *217*

Notes and Sources   *227*
Acknowledgements   *241*

Forecast

As I pick my way along the small beach, the wind strengthens up the Forth. Northeasterly weather ought to be perishing at this time of year, but instead we have the warmest February day on record; temperatures are in the high teens.

A pebble catches my eye, burnt sienna-red flecked with orange, and I stoop to feel its texture and weight. I spent years studying the language of rocks, learning to read their stories. This, though, is a fragment of brick, weathered and made round by years of pounding in the surf. Here, among the sand and grit, the pebbles of sandstone and granite, the oyster shells and limpets, are brick, concrete, pottery, bone, clinker and coal. Glass, worn smooth and opaque, catches the weak February sunlight, giving just a hint of wild sea-green. This shore speaks of the Anthropocene, the industriousness of people.

But this is not a story of stones. This is about you and how I found you – Anthony Commiskey Ford – in a place where it was forbidden to collect stones. Somehow you slipped into the deep folds of my pocket instead. I've felt the weight of you since.

You'd have played on this beach as a child, though you'd barely recognise it now. Gone are the railways, the coal and timber yards, the sewage works and the old lemonade factory that made fishcakes in the war. Now the Granton shore is an odd mix of the old and new, stuck midway on its journey to gentrification, the western half of the harbour concreted over and built up into smart waterfront flats. Alongside are derelict warehouses, old factories and the half-abandoned cement works. The once foul-smelling air carries the scent of salt-breeze and seaweed. It's a long way from the tiny island of South Georgia, where I found you in a scant grave.

I spent over two years piecing together your life, wrapping the meagre facts of you in stories, picking them up one by one as each glint caught my eye. I searched for traces of you in the south and the north and the vast blue between, but I was still one story short of making sense of you.

I have just come from meeting your friends. The men are stooped now, their hair white as sea-ice, but their camaraderie is still strong; I watched as they helped each other up the front steps of the Portobello hotel and into the tartan-carpeted bar for their annual get-together. We ate lunch overlooking the firth as they told me their well-honed stories, recounted their escapades. I'd hoped I would come away knowing all about you, but memories fade, the colours bleached dim by sun and rain, the fabric of them thin and brittle. And perhaps their memories of you are not ones they wanted to keep.

Yet still I had this image of you, as clear as the icy waters of the Weddell Sea. You are riding the lookout barrel, scouring the ocean for whales the way you combed these Granton shores for treasure as a kid. You see spouts on the horizon and raise the shout: *Hvalblåst! Whales!* The gunner gives you a thumbs-up. The engines belch smoke as the catcher wheels in the direction of the pod; the chase is on. For hours the whales are hunted to exhaustion. You see the clear waters ripple across their panicked backs as the catcher closes in. The gunner runs to the bow, his sights set on a large female blue whale. You see the young calves struggle to keep pace with the pod. You see the gunner with his finger on the trigger. You know that when he fires the harpoon, trailing its snake of blue nylon rope, it will lodge deep into her ribcage. Then the dull detonation of the grenade will follow and instantly end her life, or worse, condemn her to a long and agonising death. I could see it all so clearly. But there was one thing missing: how did you feel in that moment? What lay in your heart?

As I readied to leave the lunch, my questions unanswered, feeling you still so distant, there was Ian, in his neck brace, a walking stick clasped in both hands. He had been so quiet I'd barely noticed him. But as the old men laughed and chatted in a swirl around us, saying their farewells, perhaps the last for some, I sat wrapped in stillness as Ian told me his story. And finally, I understood your life, your death. I knew who you were.

In my hand is the Ex-Whalers Club badge. 'You're one of us now,' they said, pressing it in my palm as I left. I'll get thrown out of the vegans for this. I thumb its surface and draw back my arm to launch it into the estuary. It's time to cast you off. But something stops me.

Not yet. There are two sides to every story. And first, I need to tell yours.

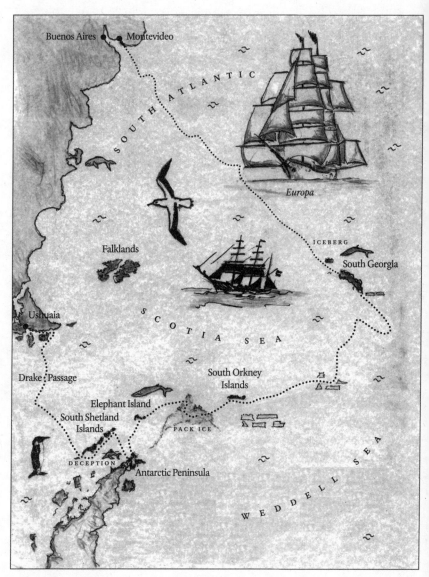

Bark *Europa* voyage, November/December 2016, Montevideo to Ushuaia via South Georgia and the Antarctic Peninsula (reproduced courtesy of Klaas Gaastra).

Part One

SOUTH

. . . in reality, our north is the south.
We don't need a north, except to oppose our south.
[. . .] This reorientation is essential; for now we know where
we are.

JOAQUÍN TORRES GARCÍA

1

Orientation

My journey to Antarctica had begun simply enough. 'I've been thinking,' I said. G rolled his eyes. These three words usually preceded some scheme to upturn our lives: kids, a change of career, a new business venture. But this time, it was personal. At fifty, I'd found myself adrift in the uncertainty of middle age, my energy as depleted as my hormones.

Six years before, I had given up a good academic career, lecturing and researching in environmental science. Despite my love of stones, I found that only through a career in oil or mining can a living be made from them; instead, I made maps. I marked territories and borders, though I soon learned that drawing lines on a map was not as simple as I'd first thought: very little is quite so clear-cut.

I left academia when it became a competitive sport, leaving me burned out and disillusioned, and built up a successful business finding suitable sites for wind-farm developers. But I was exhausted; the last twenty years had been relentless.

G put down the dish towel. 'Okay. And?'

'I've been thinking about going to Antarctica.'

'Oh. When? How will you get there? How long for?' But not why. He understood that sometimes I needed to get away.

I could hear the kids in the living room bickering over the remote control. All grown up and in their late teens, our daughter was working and our son in college.

I told G about the trip I'd found: a tall-ship voyage from Uruguay to South Georgia and the Antarctic.

'That's a relief. I thought you might be running off to join Sea Shepherd.'

I had often talked about volunteering with the activist group. Sea Shepherd had been sending ships to Antarctica every year since 2002 and used extreme and dangerous tactics to disrupt the Japanese whaling fleet still illegally hunting there. Although I struggled with the thought of *any* animal being needlessly killed, the slaughter of whales seemed to me the greatest crime of all. But much as I admired what Sea Shepherd did, I wasn't badass enough to join them.

'Will you be okay if I go?' I asked G.

'I'll be fine. I've people to phone if I need help. I promise.'

When we first met, G had occasional bouts of anxiety and low mood. At some point that I can't quite put my finger on, his anxiety got the better of him. He struggled to hold down a job. He struggled with the kids during school breaks or on family holidays. He didn't fly – it was his worst fear of all – whereas I'd spent my life travelling, my parents living abroad for more years than not, my own family now spread over three countries. With G's blessing, I began taking the kids to visit my mum in Spain for holidays. We needed time off from the tinnitus-shrill of his anxiety and left him behind in the hope that a break from us would help. I'm not so sure now it was the right thing to do. G's low spells lengthened and joined up, ceased their ebb and flow with the seasons until his depression became our way of life. And I couldn't fix it. I couldn't fix it. Sometimes it was just too damn sad, and I was in danger of being dragged under too. *Put on your own life vest first.*

I needed time at sea.

~

Anthony Commiskey Ford: at first, I'd thought your middle name Russian. Commiskey. But it's Irish. MacCumascaigh, from Longford. That's where the Ford came from. It was your grandfather that changed his name – *no Blacks, no Irish* – or maybe it was just easier on the tongue. But still there was pride there: you all had Commiskey as your middle name. That's how I tracked you down. I imagine you rolling the word around on your tongue, hissing out the S.

You were born in 1933, in a small tenement flat on Drummond Street in Edinburgh. I go there looking for your home, the place named on your birth certificate. A turning off South Bridge, vibrant and busy, leads to a quiet lane paved with granite setts. On the corner, a one-storey baroque Italian restaurant with wooden balustrades stands out of place among the tall sandstone city buildings. Your narrow terraced tene-ment is still there, the most dilapidated building on the street, the windows boarded up. It seems it was always so: over fifty people were crammed into that building, portioned up into tiny two-room flats, with little in the way of sanitation.

I stand in the street, my back to the building opposite, newly converted to flats but still with the words *boys* and *girls* carved into its pale sandstone lintels. A clacking gull passes overhead, its shadow dashing across the cobbles, and I see you, aged seven, looking out from your window, your eyes following the gull's glide over the school's verdigris turret towards the Old Infirmary, where a swivelling wind vane points its fat arrow west. The bird disappears into the distant blue of the sea, a short snatch of horizon squeezed between Edinburgh's rooftops.

There are eight of you living in that small flat. Robert, your father, takes on labouring jobs when he can, and your mother, Josephine, scrubs floors and laundry. Your grandmother, Angelina – Nana Lina – lives with you too. The daughter of an Italian piano tuner, she was born in Dublin and grew up in the Grassmarket of Edinburgh. The cheap but overcrowded lodgings there were the landing place for most migrants and those who couldn't afford a regular rent. Even Drummond Street is a step up from that hellhole.

You've two older siblings, Mary and Robert. Robert is the clever one in the family, earning his place at grammar school, passing the eleven plus, the exam designed to separate those destined for better things from those dealt a life of labour, like your father. Yet you also will not do so well. And then there are your younger brothers, Gerald and Patrick, though all your names get shortened: Robbie, Tony, Gerry and Paddy. Mary is still Mary, though.

Before Robbie takes his place at grammar school, an illness rakes through the family. Your mother thinks you sick with the flu at first, burning up with a sore throat and headache, you and your brothers sweating in your ragged shared bed for a week. Poor Paddy gets it worst. Just as he discovered the joy of exploring the world on foot, his newfound legs are stilled, no longer able to support him. He becomes listless, struggles to breathe. Your mother takes him to the Sick Children's Hospital, but it is too late. The polio has taken hold. A priest is called to give him the last rites.

Your mother, even at the age of thirty-two, has already had her fill of grief, though it doesn't make it easier. From a Northern Irish Catholic family, she worked in the flax mills from the age of twelve, one of eight children, though only five survived to adulthood. Just before the First World War, her family moved to Glasgow, and her older brother John, then nineteen, signed up to fight. Josephine was only ten when he died on the fields of Flanders less than a year later. She was eighteen when she married Robert and moved in with him and his mother Lina, herself widowed in the war. They made that small flat in Drummond Street your home. Her third child, Edward, died of bronchopneumonia when she was pregnant with you. This family so girdled in grief – it would suffocate the best of us. And yet it forged Josephine's strength. She girded you against poverty, taught you to work hard, to always do your best, to strive for something better. From such beginnings, I can understand her urgency.

~

I remember my first encounter with the wildness of the sea, the kind of maddening, tempestuous tumult that throws itself salt-foamed and raging against cliffs, harbour walls and lighthouses. There was nothing romantic about this first meeting; we were crossing the English Channel on a school day-trip to Boulogne. A storm had conjured huge waves, and vomit ran along the ferry corridors. My friend Ruth and I tried to head out to the open-air decks to escape the stench. A sympathetic steward, mop in hand, blocked our way but sent us to the below-decks lounge at the very front of the ship. 'It's the worst place to be on the boat in a storm,' he said, 'so seasick people don't go in there.'

As we walked in, a lady looked up from her paper and nodded at us. It was quiet, and those not reading snoozed. We sat with our feet up against the outslope of the hull, feeling each wave smash on the other side of the steel. Our stomachs lurched as we rose up and over each crest. It was thrilling. I was hooked.

At sea, you know where you are. You plot your position on a chart, you read the weather. The wind veers, and you tack and trim your sails, but the track of the stars and the pull of the compass are constant. You flow with the currents, cycle with the moon, adjust your balance with every wave. You know your exact place on this planet: a tiny speck of nothingness.

In my thirties, I discovered the world of classic sailing on tall ships, schooners and even trawlers – vessels restored and crewed by an eclectic and eccentric mix of people with a love of hand-crafted boats. Sailing old ships is hard graft. The voyages were not cheap, and the ships were costly to maintain, so they took on paying guest crew who were expected to work too. For me, it was the perfect escape – travelling and sailing, working with like-minded people.

I hadn't been on a voyage since the kids had come along, but now I'd found the perfect trip: South Georgia and the Antarctic, following in the footsteps of Ernest Shackleton. And I was a big fan of Shackleton.

When our children were young, we'd had a day out at Discovery Point in Dundee – my favourite place to go on a winter's day. It had been quiet, and we ran around the *Discovery*, playing pirates. I loved the feel of the wooden decks, the creaking of timbers, the way the masts pierced the sky, but I especially loved the wheel and binnacle, a snowless snow-globe housing the ship's bobbing compass – it felt like a portal to the entire planet.

In the gift shop, I'd been drawn to a book about Shackleton's failed Trans-Antarctic Expedition. On the cover was a three-masted tall ship, *Endurance*, square-rigged in a cobweb of ropes, gripped in a frozen sea. I bought the book, captivated by Frank Hurley's stunning photographs: the mountainous landscapes of South Georgia, the last port before heading south; the ice-locked ship in the Weddell Sea; the portraits of the men, grubby-faced and leathery-skinned; their daily lives on the floe waiting for the spring melt; the *Endurance* crushed like kindling in a fist of ice. The ship broke to a splintered wreck before sinking beneath the frozen sea. 'She is gone, boys,' Shackleton whispered as she slipped into the dark. The men spent months living on the ice before hauling the life-boats to open water. After a week of rowing and sailing without respite, they made landfall at the uninhabited Elephant Island, but Shackleton didn't rest long before taking five of his men into the largest lifeboat and sailing 800 miles back to South Georgia. It was an epic tale of survival, endurance and optimism, and I was in desperate need of optimism.

I would travel on the *Europa*, a three-masted Dutch barque. She was stunning. A little longer than the *Endurance*, but a little sleeker too, *Europa* had begun her life in 1911 as a light-ship vessel on the River Elbe. In the 1980s, she was taken to the Netherlands and converted to a tall ship and has wandered the world since as a sail-training vessel, with many seasonal voyages to the Antarctic under her keel.

I had a few last-minute Christmas gifts to buy before I left and made my way through the shopping centre to Lush for some stocking fillers.

'You're well organised,' the assistant said as I loaded up with the kids' favourite bath-bombs.

'Yes, it's just that I'll be away until Christmas Eve.'

'You off somewhere exciting?'

I told her about my trip, though I felt a bit of a fraud. It seemed frivolous to be travelling to such a place.

She paused packing up my things. Her eyes drifted up and out of the shop door. 'You know, I used to work in shipping, sailing container ships. I miss the sea.'

As I left the shop, I heard her running up behind me. 'Here, take this,' she said as I turned. 'It seems so perfect.' She handed me a cotton neckerchief printed with every kind of penguin. 'Have an amazing time. Come in and tell us all about it when you get back.'

And that's how it went. Friends, acquaintances and even strangers didn't think it ridiculous or frivolous. I was given all manner of portable gifts: scarves, brooches, a pop-up tall ship.

It seems this effect is universal. Early explorers discovered that departure for the Antarctic turned out to be their most successful chat-up line. Men placing personal ads in newspapers mentioning Antarctica were deluged with offers. There was clearly something about the Great White Continent that inspired a yearning to have even some small part in its story.

The day before I left, G's sister and her husband came over for lunch. I wanted them to be on hand while I was away – just in case G was struggling. We sat in the living room, letting our meal settle, chatting about my trip, my brother-in-law especially interested. He had worked most of his career on a geophysical survey boat – all seas, all weathers.

'That's a very tiny boat for such a serious ocean,' he said.

'It'll be fine.' My stock phrase. 'They sail there every year. I'm sure they know what they're doing. Besides, they have satnav and charts and weather forecasts now. It's not exactly *here be dragons* any more.'

'And you're sailing south of Cape Horn in that? That's going to be hellish scary.'

'Yes, but that's kind of the point. It needs to be a bit scary.'

'Oh, you'll be scared.'

And for the first time, I did feel nervous.

With my bags packed and stacked up in the hallway, I held up a pink plastic folder stuffed with sheets of paper, some printed, some handwritten. Our home insurance policy, emergency numbers, contact details for the ship. 'Everything you need to know is in here,' I told the family. I'd ordered weekly food deliveries, and one for Christmas too. Meal plans were pinned to the kitchen cupboard, and I'd stocked up the freezer. 'My bank account details, my will, my power of attorney in case I'm lost at sea. All in here.'

'Mum, stop panicking. We'll be fine,' said my youngest, seventeen. He couldn't understand the fuss.

My biggest fear, though, was not being lost at sea in some storm or falling from a high yardarm while stowing the sails, plummeting into the sea below with a tiny white pluff. My biggest fear was that if something happened at home while I was away, I wouldn't be able to get back.

'Not a hope. You might as well be going into outer space,' the booking agent had said when I'd asked.

~

Seven years later, and you're holding on tight to your Nana Lina as you walk along the Portobello shore. You're tall and slender now, almost a man already. The hot August weekend

11

has brought everyone down to the sea for the fresh breeze. Nana Lina is frail but can still walk a little way with help. You miss seeing her every day now that you and the family have moved out to Granton into a fancy new council flat. You've even got an indoor bathroom, as well as a kitchen, living room and two bedrooms. And best of all, from your window, the view stretches right out across the Firth of Forth, with all its changing moods and weather.

Nana Lina asks about school; she has a knack of knowing what's bothering you. You look down at the ground, not sure what to say.

'Och well, school's not for everyone, I suppose,' she replies without waiting for an answer. 'Robbie got all the brains in your family.' She leans in and whispers with a grin, 'But you got the looks.'

You're not daft, though. You love books, devour them even, but it's the maths that gets you. Numbers are as much of a mystery as the depths of the oceans.

You're having a family day out – everyone's here: your mum and dad, Nana Lina, your Aunt Lottie, Mary, Robbie, Gerry, your new brother Michael – only a year old and still in his pram – and your cousins too, though they're much older than you, more like aunts and uncles than cousins. And you're all in your Sunday best, you in your new shirt and trousers.

'It's important to always look smart,' your mum says.

You're wearing a cardigan over the top, though it's getting a little short in the sleeves. But it will do. Your mum says you'll need to start buying your own clothes soon.

'You've got to do something with your life,' she keeps telling you. 'You need to earn money.'

You do have a part-time job delivering groceries for the local Co-op, but the pay isn't much. You're nearly fifteen, old enough to leave school, and there's no point in staying, but you still don't have a proper job or apprenticeship lined up.

Further ahead, you see your cousin's husband Sammy, gathering everyone along the sea wall for a photo. He's got one of those fancy new Kodak cameras. He beckons to you and Nana Lina to join the group. She's edged into the middle, and you sit up on the sea wall at the back.

'Smile for the camera,' Sammy says, clicking the shutter. It's the first time you've had your picture taken, and you sit stiff-limbed and uncertain as the moment is captured.

As everyone begins to disperse, Sammy catches your eye and nods for you to come over. You're about to jump down from the wall when he raises the camera again. You grin widely as he takes your photo.

'You want to see how this works?' he asks. You're fascinated and listen intently as he explains how to measure the light, how to set the exposure, where to put in the film and how to look through the lens and focus it. He even lets you take a couple of photos.

'I got it when I was away whaling,' he tells you. 'They have a shop on board the ship, and you can buy just about anything you want: cameras, fancy watches, chocolates, clothes, all sorts. You don't even pay for it at the time. The store man just ticks it off, and they take it out of your wages at the end of the season.'

You can't imagine being able to buy something as fancy as a watch or a camera.

'Your mum says you're looking for a job,' Sammy says. 'Have you thought about going whaling? It's hard work right enough, but even on the lowest wages it's good money. And with your birthday next month you'll be just in time for this year's season. I can put in a good word for you with

13

Salvesen's if you like? I'm sure they'd take you on as a mess boy.'

You know lads from your school who went whaling last year, working for Salvesen as mess boys, coming back in the spring after their first season, strong and healthy-looking, flashing their cash, zooming around on new motorbikes, the girls flocking round them to hear their tales. You had to do something with your life, *make a man of yourself*, as your dad would say, and you've always loved the idea of going to sea.

Two weeks later, you're standing with your dad in a plush room upstairs at the Salvesen offices on Bernard Street in Leith, waiting to get called in for an interview with one of the managers. It's a busy place: men dressed in suits puff on pipes, dash around with bits of paper or sit at desks talking on telephones. Women in smart skirts and tailored jackets clack at typewriters. Your dad shuffles foot to foot, in his best suit.

'Anthony Ford.' The manager calls you in, but he doesn't invite you to sit. You stand in front of his desk feeling like you're in the headmaster's office at school.

'So, you'll be fifteen next month?' he asks. You nod. 'And you want to go whaling?' You nod again. He turns to your dad. 'And you're his father, I take it? You're happy to give your permission?' It's your father's turn to nod.

'Well, we've got a recommendation from your cousin. He says you're a hard worker and you look tall and strong enough. You ever been to sea before?' You shake your head. 'Not much to say for himself, has he?'

Your father smiles. 'No, he's a quiet lad, but he'll work hard.'

'Aye, well, he'll need to.'

The manager signs you on for the *Southern Venturer* as a mess boy, working in the ship's galley. You'll help prepare meals and serve the men. The job is seven days a week, but you'll get paid double-time on a Sunday and your wages will be 6 pounds, 10 shillings a month. As accommodation and food is included, there won't be much to spend it on when you're away, plus you'll get your bonus at the end of the season if the ship meets its target. You agree to leave your mum 30 shillings a month out of your wages – she can pick it up at the office every fortnight.

You're pleased at the thought of being able to earn money for the family. Maybe your dad won't have to work so hard.

'Come back a week on Wednesday – you'll need a medical before you go. I'll take you downstairs to meet Pat. She'll sort out your train ticket down to Newcastle.'

As you walk down the stairs, the leaded stained-glass window on the landing catches your eye. Small latticed panes surround a circular panel depicting St George slaying the dragon, and around it are the words THE SOUTH GEORGIA COMPANY LIMITED. Below it, another panel shows a curvy Viking ship with a dragon's head and tail at either end. You stop to get a closer look at the words on a ribboned scroll above it: INVENI PORTUM. Robbie would know what it means. The manager sees you looking.

'It's from a Latin motto,' he says. 'My ship is safe in port.'

'Damn right their ship is safe in port,' your dad says to you under his breath as you follow the manager downstairs. 'I bet this lot never go to sea.'

~

I flew out to Uruguay in early November, landing in Montevideo in the early hours of the morning and travelling from the airport by taxi through smart suburbs to Ciudad

Vieja, the old town. The man I awoke at the hotel – hastily attired in vest and braces – took time to fetch me a bottle of cold water from the fridge and show me how everything in the room worked. I was touched by his bleary-eyed efforts to make me feel welcome but relieved to flop down on the bed as soon as he'd left.

When I woke later, the warmth of the day was already seeping into the airy room. The Hotel Palacio stood on a side street, opposite a derelict two-storey building made of creamy stone. My narrow balcony looked straight into its empty upper floor, where the morning sunlight flooded through holes in the roof. I couldn't tell what it had once been. It seemed there were many buildings like this in the old town: too expensive to maintain, too beautiful to demolish.

In a leafy square filled with chittering sparrows, I break-fasted on strong coffee and toast at a café with red plastic tables and chairs, *Coca-Cola* scrawled across them in white. It felt good to be travelling alone again, not having to think too hard about where we might eat to satisfy our diverse family tastes. I began to feel a little lighter.

A market was setting up – antiques, bric-a-brac and hand-crafted souvenirs – though the stall holders seemed in no rush to get going. They stopped to chat and drink from small bulbous gourds topped-up from thermos flasks tucked under their armpits like the morning paper. I bought post-cards and a few small souvenirs for the kids and wandered the streets.

The walls of the old town were bright with murals: a square-faced cat with six purple eyes, tangerine pueblos in violet mountains, ragged fabrics stretched like spiders' webs across boarded-up windows. The houses, tall and balconied, had the most beautiful doors – thick, centuries old, wood worn to ridges along the grain. Gargoyle-knocked, iron-hinged and handled, they opened onto the narrow cobbled lanes.

It was easy to fall in love with Uruguay, a laid-back place with a hint of its revolutionary past – art, live music, tango in leafy squares, markets, artists and bohemians ready to rebel if it weren't for the warmth of the afternoon sun, and the fact that they now had little to rebel against. It seemed a country comfortable in its own skin. The flag, with its ever-shining sun and sea-blue stripes, fluttered high over every official building.

I'm awkward and reticent around those I don't know well, so I'd reached out to a few of the other guest crew in advance. In the late afternoon, I made my way to the Plaza Independencia to meet Kate at a hotel.

The plaza, separating the old and new parts of the city, is entered through a crumbling gateway, the only remaining part of the old-town wall. In its centre stands a statue of José Gervasio Artigas mounted on his horse, surrounded by tall palm trees. Artigas fought fiercely against both British and Spanish colonialism and is a national hero, known as the father of Uruguayan nationhood.

I was a little early, so I descended the stone steps below the statue into the cool cavernous space of Artigas's underground tomb. It felt calm and quiet in contrast to the busy plaza; tourists spoke in reverential whispers and softened their footsteps. In the centre, an enormous urn sat in a pool of sunlight, flanked by military guards. Directly above it, on the busy plaza, a truncated pyramid, open at the top, spilled daylight down onto Artigas's remains.

On the southern edge of the plaza, an immaculate turquoise 1955 Chevrolet Bel Air sat parked at the entrance to Kate's hotel. I found her inside at the bar, petitely perched on a stool and sipping a tall flute of champagne. She slipped down to greet me with a hug and ordered me a drink.

I looked round at the cool marble floors and elegant furnishings. 'What a beautiful place.'

'Yes, I thought it best to book in somewhere a bit more upmarket as I'm on my own. Rather lovely, isn't it? I've arranged to meet Peter here too. He should be along soon.'

Peter was one of the Dutch passengers. I hadn't met him in person, but we had connected on Facebook.

'So, what brings you on this trip?' She swivelled around on her stool and looked at me over the rim of her glass. I told her that I had fancied doing something a bit adventurous. That I needed time on my own and that I was a big fan of Shackleton. Kate was much the same. She thought she needed a 'bit of a push' at her time of life.

'It all feels a bit daunting at the moment, though,' she confessed. 'I haven't sailed much.'

'I used to, years ago, but these days I'm mostly confined to watching *Deadliest Catch*.'

The television programme was my guilty secret. My family thought it hilarious that a vegan could be addicted to a programme about Alaskan crab fishing. But I was drawn in by the drama, the epic sea-states and the fierce camaraderie of the crews working together for a percentage share in the catch. Kate, it turned out, loved the programme too.

As we chatted, Peter arrived. He strode towards us, tall, slim and greying, with a smile that took over his whole face, and greeted us like long-lost friends. Peter was instantly likeable.

Over the following days, we gathered as guest crew from Australia, New Zealand, North America and Europe, exploring the city together with regular rests for cold beer. I began to feel more at ease with my fellow travellers. On the afternoon before we sailed, we dispersed for a little time to ourselves before meeting again for an evening meal, and I went off to visit the Museo Torres García. A poster in the window had caught my eye.

Housed in a tall narrow building, the museum stood on a smart cobbled street. Displayed large in the window was a drawing of South America by Joaquín Torres García. Though born in Uruguay, the artist spent much of his life living abroad. When he returned in 1935, he created *América Invertida*: a map of South America with its tip pointing towards the top of the page.

Maps nearly always include some kind of bias and have been at the heart of politics for centuries. The world maps that adorned the classroom walls when I was a child nearly always used the Mercator projection, a method of translating the globe onto a flat sheet of paper and designed for navigating oceans, but this type of projection exaggerates the size of countries lying at higher latitudes, minimising those nearer the equator. The distortion suited the empire builders of Europe, giving them an inflated view of their own self-importance.

Torres García's *América Invertida* was a strong political statement. It shows the continent on its own terms, not just as a poor relation to North America. *Who is to say which way is up?* it brazenly asks in its deceptively simple lines. And he placed Uruguay right at its heart, at the centre of the page, where the equator would normally be. On the top left of his map, a three-masted tall ship sailed under a bright sun; on the top right was the Southern Cross under a waxing moon. I bought a postcard of it and wrote on the back: *The South is now our North. See you all at Christmas. Love Mum xxx*

That evening, we ate our last land-based meal together near the port. I sat at the end of a long table filled with platters of food. I'd refused the meat and fish. Bill, a thin wiry man, Australian, late sixties maybe, was sitting to my right.

'Oh, so you're one of those bloody leftie tree-huggers, are you?'

'Well, yes, I suppose I am,' I replied, not sure how serious he was.

'Thought so. You're the sort that tells us not to fly or burn coal. It's a load of bloody nonsense all this global warming, if you ask me.'

I shouldn't take the bait. The restaurant felt hot and busy, waiters squeezing sideways between chairs, armfuls of plates piled high with food. I looked across the table to Kate for back-up, but she was deep in conversation with Peter, his face dancing a jig of expressions.

'It's all bullshit. It's just one big conspiracy theory. You don't believe it all, do you? The information is all there on the Internet. You should look into it.'

I'd spent my entire career drifting around all things environmental, but never quite saved the planet as I'd planned. I still took it personally when people scorned the science, though. Deniers have a key weapon – they play on the very thing that makes science science: uncertainty. I hadn't the stomach for this. What was I doing, about to go to the arse-end of the planet with all these people I didn't know? I should be at home. I stared down at my food.

I woke the following morning feeling stronger, further bolstered by a last video call to the family. My son looked tired, just out of bed even though they were three hours ahead, but I was pleased to see his pale face. My daughter was at work already.

'How do I get in to my email again?' G asked.

'It's all in the manual,' I reminded him. The cat, hearing my voice, brushed against the laptop, purring.

~

In a small room upstairs in Salvesen's office in Bernard Street, Robertson, the doctor, conducts his medical examinations. Along the corridor outside, a line of chairs fills with a ragtag assortment of men waiting to see him. Here are the captains, officers, bosuns, engineers, stewards, technicians, electricians, plumbers, butchers, bakers, radio-men and, evident among them all for their startled faces, the young first-time mess boys, like you.

You're on your own today, determined to be a man already, and as nervous as that makes you feel, you're glad of it. It wouldn't have done to turn up with your dad – you'd never have heard the last of it.

'Look, here's another young 'un ready for sacrifice on the Southern Ocean,' a rough-looking man in a flat cap jeers.

You take a seat at the end of the queue next to a huge man in a navy sweater and the double-breasted, high-collared woollen jacket of a sailor. He extends a meaty hand and tells you his name is McGovern. He's the bosun on the *Southern Venturer*.

'Dinnae mind that lot,' he says, 'they're only teasing. First trip?'

You nod as your hand is lost within his. You want to ask what a bosun does, but before you get the words out, there's a

21

commotion of loud greetings and exclamations following a tall man as he strides down the corridor.

'Ah, here's Ferguson. Didn't think it'd be long before he turned up,' says McGovern. 'He's the manager on the *Venturer*. Mind and keep in with him. Most important man on the ship, aside from the captain. He can make or break our bonuses at the end of the season.'

Ferguson, dressed in a long cashmere coat and Homburg hat, walks along the line, shaking the hands of each man in turn. He greets them all by name and asks after their children and wives.

'New mess boy, are you?' He grabs your hand in both of his. 'Welcome, welcome. Don't look so worried, lad. We'll look after you, won't we, boys?' The men nod in your direction as you feel your cheeks redden.

Ferguson turns to the rest of the men. 'Have you met the new doctor yet? Saw him in the bar yesterday. Lord, we'll have fun with this one, boys. Thinks he's fucking Ishmael.' The men bellow with laughter as he heads to the front of the queue.

'Then you must be my Queequeg.' The doctor opens his office door, grinning. 'Come in, Ferguson, let's have a look at you.'

McGovern leans in to answer your question before you've even asked it. 'Characters in *Moby-Dick*. You should read it if you're going to be a whaler.'

The chat and laughter go on inside the room for a good twenty minutes as the men sit shuffling outside. Finally Ferguson bursts from the door. 'C'mon, boys. The doc says that if you've had a drink you'd better come back tomorrow morning before the bars open. He wants you sober for your medical.' Most of the men get up and turn to go, and Ferguson

22

breezes out as he breezed in. 'Lunch is on me, boys. I've had a win on the horses.'

Now that most of the men have left, it doesn't take long before it's your turn. The doctor is tall and efficient, dressed in the checked-shirt-and-tweed-jacket combination favoured by country gentlemen. He talks like one too, but he seems kind enough, and interested. You strip down to your underwear, and he puts the cold stethoscope to your chest, peers into your ears and down your throat, looks at your teeth.

'You'll do,' he pronounces, signing your papers with a flourish. It's all over in a few minutes. You dress and make your way downstairs to pick up your train ticket. You're to leave on Monday morning.

And then you're out on the pavement, feeling a little dazed. It's all happened so fast. You walk home past your school. Some of your former classmates are outside the gates having a sneaky cigarette. Being the oldest in your year, you're one of the first to leave. As your friends gather round to hear your news, you find yourself putting on a bit of a swagger, boasting about going to the Antarctic and telling them how much you'll earn. Even the girls are interested in you all of a sudden. You head home, full of confidence.

'Get yourself up to Nana Lina's,' your mum says when you get in. 'She's got something for you.'

Nana Lina now lives in a small flat near the centre of town with Aunt Lottie, who lost her husband a few years ago. Lottie is getting old too, nearly seventy, but she's still fit and active, with Nana Lina's glint in her eye. You've no money for the bus fare but prefer to walk anyway. It's a sunny day, and you stride out, thinking about your classmates stuck indoors at school. Nana Lina greets you with a tighter hug than usual and gathers you inside. The flat is small but clean. A bright bay window overlooks the street, and you can smell fresh baking from the kitchenette.

Lottie appears with a pale patterned china plate filled with shortbread and a bottle of Trussell's ginger beer for you, a rare treat.

'Tell us about your new job, then,' says Nana Lina. You unfold the story of the posh Salvesen offices, thick with pipe smoke, telephones and typewriters. You tell them about your interview and medical, about the new doctor and Ferguson the manager, and how all the drunk men went off with him for lunch. You show them your train ticket down to Newcastle.

'I bet you're nervous about it all, but you'll be fine,' Nana Lina says. 'You're a good strong lad and a hard worker and that's all you need to be. Keep your head down and do what you're told. Sammy says the men'll look out for you, keep you right.'

'What about clothes? You'll need something warm to wear. It'll be cold,' Lottie says.

You tell them how you can buy everything on the ship and it just gets taken out your wages at the end of the trip. Nana Lina looks across to Lottie, who nods and goes through to the bedroom, returning with a long army trench coat.

'Here you go, son, take this. It was your Uncle Tommy's, and he'd be proud for you to have it. C'mon, stand up and try it on.' Lottie slips the heavy coat onto your shoulders. It smells of mothballs and baking. 'Och, it's a little big, but it'll do you fine,' she says, smoothing it down. She gathers herself to stem the tears. 'Oh, and I've made you some of your favourite tablet to take.' She disappears into the kitchen and returns with a brown paper bag.

'It'll keep, so save it for when you're away and need reminding of home.'

As you stand at the door ready to leave, Nana Lina draws you in for an even tighter hug. 'You've always been my favourite, you know that,' she whispers in your ear. And though you know she says it to your brothers and your sister too, you also know she means it. Nana Lina makes you all feel special. She draws away to cup your face in her hands.

'Now mind and look after yourself. And make sure you come back safe and sound.'

2

Navigation

Peter and I shared a taxi to the port. The dockside felt noisy and hazardous, full of multi-coloured containers stacked like Lego. Forklifts beeped and zipped between them. We found *Europa* hidden among the colossal ships and fishing factories; she seemed out of time and place in this industrial setting. Compared to the rusting hulks around her, she was sleek, beautiful, hand-built – and tiny. The top of her tall masts barely reached deck level of the ships around her.

We bundled aboard, and overstuffed bags disappeared through hatches and down steep steps to the cabins below. I was pleased to see I'd be sharing with Kate. She gave me a tour of the small wood-panelled cabin, the clever nooks and crannies where we could stow our things: varnished lockers and drawers with flush brass handles. The bunks, extra-long for the Dutch, could be made private by drawing a navy-blue cotton curtain across them. Survival suits hung on straps above each bunk. I felt more settled seeing my space for the next six weeks.

On the morning of the November full moon, we sailed from Montevideo. As we left port, the so-called Cemetery of Ships flanked our starboard side like an upturned box of toys.

Tilted close-knit wrecks lay abandoned by dint of debts or liens, some just plain rusted and forgotten, though many of the vessels in port were barely more seaworthy. Far out on the wide Río de la Plata estuary, fleets of anchored reefer ships – refrigerated vessels – peeked their cranes and bridges over the horizon, their decks hidden behind the curvature of the Earth. The seas off Uruguay are rich in life and attract unregulated fishing boats from across Asia and Europe. Catches are offloaded to reefer ships at sea, and when the fish arrives in Montevideo, though the captains declare its origins, checks are virtually impossible.

The wind veered in our favour, and the crew loosened *Europa*'s sails to the breeze. The silty estuarine hue turned sharp lapis blue, and our phones lost signal. We would see no more land nor ships for twelve days. It felt odd but liberating to disconnect from the rest of the world, to sail away and leave it all behind.

Deep within the ship that first night, I sensed the swirl of movement around me: the gush of water, the sound of bubbles streaking the underside of our hull, people, footsteps, ropes dropping onto the deck above. My berth lay right at the heart of the ship, at the root of the main mast. We slept below the waterline, our porthole a pale blue washing machine rinsing through our dreams. I felt the rise and fall of the ocean, lulled on my giant waterbed. I let go, lost the boundaries of myself to the ship, and my breath slowed to the rhythm of the long ocean swell. I stirred only when I felt a shift in the wind tugging through our sails, pulling me forward in my sleep.

On board, twenty permanent crew and forty guests packed the tiny cabins. I wandered a little aimless on the first day, not yet attuned to the daily cadence of the ship. I recognised the same lost look in my crew-mate Heikki, a droll and raspy

28

Dutchman. Whenever I found a quiet spot, he would be there already or soon follow behind. We'd both signed on for the wild solitude of the Antarctic but had perhaps overlooked the fact that we'd be on board a small ship with fifty-nine other people.

The wood-panelled deckhouse was our hub for company or something to do. 'Who wants a job?' Emma the bosun would shout, striding in with weathered wooden blocks from the rigging and a pile of sandpaper. The cook heaved in huge basins of potatoes for us to peel. On deck, a vast web of ropes furled and unfurled the sails, raised the yards and braced them to the wind. The crew drilled us in easing, sweating, coiling, heaving, making fast and belaying – the language of tall ships trawled from my memory as my hands roughened to the thick hemp ropes. We learned the sheets, bunts, clews, gaskets and halyards. We had crib sheets naming all twenty-four sails and the ropes attached to them: around 225 in total, all neatly coiled onto wooden pin rails running the length of the ship.

'Okay, listen up. Here's the rota for Red Watch,' said Heikki, nominated to take charge of our watch. He slipped a printed spreadsheet under the clear sticky laminate covering of the deckhouse tables. It detailed our every move over the next three days. Heikki was an engineer.

On watch, we rotated a cycle of lookout on the bow, steering at the helm and handling sails when called for, though the lookout and helm jobs, given the on-board radar and auto-pilot, were mostly to make us feel useful. We soon adjusted to the regular rhythm of our shifts: four hours on, eight off. At night, each watch was to wake the next. Kate's preceded mine, and she was a master of the gentle rouse. 'It's the most gorgeous night, so many stars,' she would whisper into the

dark of my bunk, or, 'You must come and see the phosphores-
cence in the ship's wake – it's incredible.' Days and nights
ceased to matter. Our lefts and rights too, replaced by port
and starboard, our bodies now a part of this ship as she
creaked and groaned her way south.

For three days, we slogged against a heavy swell, the sails
raised, lowered and raised again, trying to make the best of
the fickle wind. Mostly, we headed south under engine as the
ship wallowed in sloppy seas. Meals meant one hand on our
plates and one on our forks, plus a foot braced against something fixed and solid. Showering, when we bothered, in the
small cubicle off our cabin, felt like being in a gift-wrapped
box rattled by a curious kid. Under sail, though, the ship was
at her most glorious: six creamy broad swathes of mottled and
patched canvas stacked into the sky on the main mast, the
triangular jibs stretched from the bowsprit, honey-tinted in
the evening sun.

It felt good to be back at sea again. No responsibility, no
distractions, no emails or Internet, no meals to plan, no
housework, no commuting and no job to do other than hard
physical graft. I could feel my shoulders beginning to drop
from around my ears.

As we sailed south, the air turned cooler, the days lengthened and the midday sun burned to the north. We learned to
ride the rise and fall of the deck in the stilted wide-legged
walk of sailors. The night watches became my favourite, the
stars unfamiliar except those on the inky horizon. Orion the
Hunter breech-birthed into the pitch-black sky, his head
dangling into the sea. Venus slung a long streak of light across
our dark disk of ocean.

'You can steer by the Southern Cross tonight,' our captain
Klaas said as Heikki and I took our place at the helm. 'We're

heading due south. There she is. Line the foremast up with her.'

Steering meant constant adjustment of the ship's wheel in time to the rhythm of the swell. The foremast rose and fell like a fiddler's bow against the backdrop of the Southern Cross.

'This is the life, is it not?' Heikki filled his lungs, and we stood taking it all in. The spectacle of the night got the better of us, though, and we veered in the wrong direction. Klaas, sea-scarred, wild-haired and bearded, popped up like a prairie dog from the wheelhouse where he'd been monitoring our progress to ask in his gravelly voice, 'Remind me what heading we are meant to be on?'

~

Edinburgh Waverley station feels frantic, the aloof tones of the station announcer drowned out by the hiss of steam and clatter. The thick smog confuses you. You've never been on a train before, and you're not sure where to go. Uncle Tommy's overcoat feels too heavy and hot, and you clutch at the small battered cardboard suitcase lent to you by a kind neighbour. A wiry young lad approaches with a broad grin, a canvas duffel bag slung over his shoulder and a flat cap tipped back on his head. He asks if you're going whaling. 'I saw you at the Salvesen office,' he says. 'I'm Danny.' He grips your hand in a firm shake, 'Danny Anderson. C'mon, I'll see you right.'

Danny leads you through the throng of the station and onto the train. You make your way along the narrow corridor and into a compartment with a couple of spare seats. Danny stows his bag and jacket on the luggage rack above the seats and reaches over to open the window. 'Let's get some fresh air in here,' he says with a confidence out of kilter with his youth.

Doors clunk shut as the last passengers climb aboard, and the train groans out of the station. Soon, the sea flanks your left side, slate blue under a clear sky. Just past Berwick, Danny leans across. 'Look out for our ship. You can often see her funnels as we get near Newcastle.' Sure enough, before long, you see the South Shields shipyards and a pair of distinctive red, white and blue funnels towering above them.

Newcastle is cold and dirty, the once thriving shipyards empty of workers, steel now a rationed commodity. The *Southern Venturer*, moored on a splay of hawsers, looms above the docks. She seems bigger even than the giant gas tanks on the Granton shore but is painted in the same pale battleship-grey, rust-red around her waterline. She is long, flat and blunt-nosed like an oil tanker. Three tiers of white decks are stacked above her stern, crowned by two fat funnels side by side. A white lattice gateway of steel crosses her midships, and a tall blocky bridge, unhampered by any notions of sleek design, sits above her bow. But it's her rear slipway that marks her as a whaler: the long slope from the waterline up to the plan deck designed for winching whales aboard.

The smell hits you: the reek of rotten flesh, fish guts and rancid oil, like the long-dead seagull you once found by the shore at home, its flesh the consistency of custard. But this smell is worse and claws at the back of your nose and throat – it's the unmistakable stench of a whale ship. You can't imagine how bad it will be on board.

'Stinks, doesn't she?' Danny says, slapping you on the back. 'Don't worry, you'll get used to it.' You think it unlikely. Danny peels off to greet friends. Alongside the ship, you report to the officer in charge, and he directs you to the chief steward. After clambering the steep gangplank, you emerge onto the vast open deck, wooden and pale, but stained with the dark-russet blemish of blood.

'Off to war, are you?' A stooped man, grey as a faded photograph, gestures towards your khaki trench coat. He introduces himself as the chief steward. He checks your details and shows you to a tiny cabin at the aft of the ship, right above the engines. There are four bunks, and the two lower ones are already claimed by bags, so you place your suitcase on an upper one.

Danny arrives and slings his kitbag on the last bunk. You feel relieved to be sharing with him. 'C'mon, I'll show you round,' he says.

Danny is a wealth of information, a whaler for three years already, now working on the catchers. He seems to know everything about the ship and greets most of the men by name.

The *Southern Venturer* is truly a floating factory, a whole shore-based whale-oil refinery crammed onto a ship. Below the main deck are boilers and cookers the size of trucks, oil extractors, pipes, dehydrators, separators, pump rooms and electric conveyor belts. Deep in the hull are the thirty-two storage tanks, 620 tons of capacity in each – 20,000 in all. Twin steam engines fill the stern alongside a huge evaporator plant making 600 tons of fresh water a day. The machinery fills just about every available space, and you squeeze through the narrow gaps on the walkways.

'Don't come this way when there's a cook on,' Danny tells you. 'It's lethal with all these scalding pipes and steam.'

The *Southern Venturer* is still relatively new, built in 1945 at the end of the war, the rationed steel to build her and her sister ship, the *Southern Harvester*, authorised by Churchill himself,

Danny tells you. Whaling is crucial to Britain's recovery from the war effort, crucial to the supply of food. Most of the Salvesen ships had been commandeered for the war, and many were lost, along with the whalers that crewed them.

Over the next few days, the *Southern Venturer* fills with men returning fresh for the season, greeting each other with firm handshakes and gentle jibes. You meet your other two cabin-mates, mess boys too, but each with a couple of years' experience under their belts. They're boisterous, but they seem okay.

The next day, you start work, familiarise yourself with the job. You've to serve in the whalers' mess, the largest mess, and where most of the unskilled men eat. Your job is to lay out the cutlery, make the tea and coffee, serve the men and clean up afterwards. Between meals, you help in the galley, peeling vegetables and making soup. Not all the men have arrived yet, so it's easy work so far, but you're kept busy, and you're glad of it, enjoying your new role.

The night before the ship sails, Danny takes you across the river on the ferry to the Northumberland Arms, more affectionately known as 'The Jungle', the haunt of all sailors in North and South Shields. Rough and ready, the building houses a bar on the ground floor, a lounge on the first floor and a nightclub in the basement. The band bashes out covers of all the latest songs from Vaughn Monroe, Bing Crosby, Steve Conway and Doris Day on a tuneless piano and banjo through a smog of cigarette smoke and profanities. Since the early days of Arctic whaling, whale men have built a fearsome reputation for their shore exploits in port, especially for their wild drinking on evenings before departure. It's a lot to live up to.

Danny buys you a pint. It's your first drink, and you feel

yourself relax, laughing along with the others, joining in with their jokes, almost chatty. The other lads tease you about your trench coat. 'Eh, lads, we'll be okay – he'll defend us if it kicks off later.' A second pint arrives and slips down easily, but when a third lands on the table in front of you, the room begins to feel like it's full of treacle, not entirely unpleasant, but viscous and slow. You reach for your glass but knock it over – it spills across the table and into the lap of one of the other lads. He leaps up, cursing you. 'Get back to the ship if you can't handle your drink,' he shouts. You look for Danny, but he's away talking to a man at the bar. It's too loud and hot, so you leave, go outside and feel the cool air and the sudden quiet. You catch the ferry back over the Tyne. Halfway across, you tear off your coat, throw it in the river and watch it float away in the wake.

Later that night, the deck floods with men singing, wrapped around each other arm in arm, hugging half-empty bottles. Some lean over the rails to part with their supper. The racket lasts until the early hours, and you hide in your bunk, pulling the covers over your head, listening to the shouts and fights outside, unable to sleep, terrified. You desperately want to pack your bag and go home, but what would the family say? The other lads arrive back drunk and switch on the bright cabin lights. You pretend to be asleep.

'Are you still alive?' one asks. 'What a fucking lightweight!'

'Leave him alone,' you hear Danny saying.

~

As we slipped off the edge of the South American continental shelf, the wind jostled with sea birds. The upwelling currents surfaced an abundance of life. I leaned on the stern rails as we brisked along at eight knots, a strong wind behind us ballooning the straining sails. Though it's only a little over nine miles an hour, eight knots on a ship feels swift.

I pointed out a bird to Lex, our guide. 'It's so tiny. Has it been blown offshore?'

'A Wilson's storm petrel. Don't be fooled by them,' he said, peering through his binoculars. 'They're quite at home here.' We watched as the bird flitted over huge waves like a tiny sparrow. As it neared the sea surface, an undercarriage of gangly legs dropped, opening into wide webbed feet that dabbled at the water as the bird fed.

'There, a black-browed albatross,' said Lex.

Scythe-shaped wings tilted a little to slow the bird's flight as it cast an eye over us, its silhouette mirrored in the fierce black brow. It barely twitched a muscle to hang in the air alongside us, its belly as white and soft as bog cotton, the tops of the wings smudged a pale sooty grey. It lifted a leg to scratch behind its ear, arrogant of gravity, then, with a tiny shift of its wing, it continued the length of the ship before arcing off our bow.

We saw another albatross with a fishing hook poking from the side of its beak and dangling a line of nylon thread.

'That one had a lucky escape. They follow the tuna-fishing boats,' said Lex, running a hand through his teasel-spiked grey hair. 'They see the lures in the water and think they're fish, but then they get hooked, dragged underwater and drown.'

It seemed an undignified end for such a dignified creature that can live for well over sixty years. It's not just fishing that threatens the albatross: invasive rats prey on their eggs, and ocean plastics fill their stomachs. The plastics are often passed on to the chicks as the parents regurgitate their catch to feed them. Nineteen of the twenty-two species of albatross are now threatened, vulnerable or endangered, and two are critically endangered.

I spent many hours watching albatross from the stern rails. They are creatures of the wind, listening to every nuance of airflow with their entire bodies. In humans, we call it proprioception – the ability to know where our bodies are in space – relying on sensors in the muscles of our feet and ankles, but a lifetime of walking on pavements and flat floors has diminished our ability to the point where we don't *hear* the ground any more. Like the albatross, though, sailors listen with their entire bodies. They know the rise and fall of the ocean, sensing the sudden feeling of lightness as the ship falls away into the trough of a wave, the heaviness of riding up the crests.

Albatross hone their mastery over the millions of miles they fly in a lifetime, and the stormier the better. Higher winds require less effort – just a minute twitch of a muscle to change direction, to rise and fall over a long swell. Sometimes – and I think they did it just for fun – I'd see them trailing their wingtips through the conchoidal slick of curling waves. They seemed at their most Zen when the wind howled about them. In the doldrums, they sat bobbing in the sea, grounded and disgruntled until the wind picked up enough for them to ride the air again.

The weather worsened over the following days, and the ship shuddered and jolted south under engine with a few staysails hoisted to ease her rolling. Out on deck, lines were set up, criss-crossing the ship for us to clip on our harnesses as we stood on watch.

In the wood-panelled library at the stern of the ship sat a laptop fixed to a bench. One foot braced against the table leg, we'd use this to communicate with home, our brief messages sent by satellite phone. In a stifling economy of words, I tried to convey the vastness of the ocean, the crust of salt that clung to everything, the toothpaste-fresh hue of the waves, the constant grinding motion of the ship. In return, my inbox blinked words from home that rarely varied.

All well here. Kids fine. Hope you're enjoying your trip. G xx

It was not a lot to go on, but it would have to do. It meant he was coping; if he wasn't, the messages would have been longer. But I missed hearing about their daily lives.

On the third night of the storm, I wedged myself into my bunk with spare clothes, but we were hit by some hard waves, and the ship lurched and listed, threatening to throw us from our beds. We'd been warned to stow everything away – socks high, cameras low – but it didn't stop the regular crashing of things to the floor. Waves flooded over the rails, washing knee-deep across the decks, spilling out through the gunnels. The largest staysail was ripped clean in two by a ferocious gust of wind. But I felt safe in this old ship with her capable crew.

Kate woke me for my shift. 'Time to get up,' she mumbled before dropping her waterproofs to the floor and falling into her bunk still dressed. The weather was taking its toll on us all. Even those with the hardiest of stomachs felt exhausted. We'd barely seen some of the other guest crew for days, as they lay sick in their beds. We took them water and food, but most had little appetite.

Though I didn't suffer from seasickness, the constant churning of the ship had turned my stomach to a tight knot of indigestion, and I was beginning to feel ill with it. I pulled on my clothes: thermals, fleeces, thick trousers, waterproofs, hat, gloves and harness. The wind, now brutally cold, exploited every chink in our clothing, so we wore as much as we had. By the time I climbed up to the deckhouse, I felt faint.

'You look bloody awful,' said Bill as I slumped into a seat and dropped my head to the table.

'I feel bloody awful.'

'Go on, go back to your bunk, I'll take your shifts.'

'But you'd have to do double.'

'It's okay. I'll cover for you.'

'Even though I'm a leftie tree-hugger?' I lifted my head from the table.

He laughed. 'Yes, even for you. Now go and get some sleep.'

The next day I emerged to a bright morning and fresh seas. The air nipped hard, but the wind had eased, the clear skies full of glorious gliding seabirds. The deck was busy with folk glad to escape their stuffy cabins for the crisp air, and every-one seemed cheery again.

'Sandy!' Peter greeted me with a broad grin. 'Are you feel-ing better this morning? Have you had your coffee?'

'Yes, thanks, it's beginning to kick in.' I squeezed in beside him to sit in the sun with my toast. It felt good to be around someone so dependably cheerful. At home, I felt a constant need to lift the mood for the sake of the kids, even when I didn't feel like it myself. It had been a way of life for so long that I hadn't understood how much of a grind it had become. 'Bill was a star,' I told Peter. 'He took all my shifts.'

'He's a good man, Bill. He used to be in the navy. I think he really misses it.'

The engineers were hauling something heavy onto the deck and strapping it down. I nodded in their direction. 'What are they up to?'

'Big sewing machine for the sail repairs. It's incredible. They have everything they need to fix this old girl up.' We watched as four people worked the machine, feeding the heavy sailcloth through it.

As I lay in my bunk that afternoon, Kate burst in through the cabin door: 'Iceberg!' she shouted, scrabbling around for her camera. 'Come and see!' As I climbed out on deck, the salt spray stung my eyes. The ship, sailing close-haul on small staysails, heeled to port, where a slab of ice hung crooked on the horizon, its top edge sharp as a paper cut. Gunmetal seas lapped around its pale skirts, and small cyan caves glowed along the tideline like a jewelled hem. Where the waves fell to reveal its underbelly, the ice was moulded and softened into smooth curves.

The rails were a chatter of delight and clicking cameras, but we didn't stay long outside; the wind was perishing and the sea choppy. Instead, we sat out the afternoon in the deck-house with mugs of coffee, watching the iceberg glide by through steamy windows.

'Are you missing home?' Kate asked me.

'Do you know, I'm not,' I said. 'I miss seeing the kids, but I didn't realise how much I needed this.' I told her about G's mental-health issues.

'That's shit,' she said.

And with those two words, I knew she got it. She said the one thing I wanted to hear. The thing that nobody ever says, not on its own anyway, not without tagging on a volley of well-meant advice on SAD lamps, CBT, cannabis oil, gut bacteria, exercise, St John's Wort, acupuncture, magnesium, mindfulness, fluoxetine, sertraline, mescaline, fire-walking, rebirthing, reflexology, yoga, turmeric, turkey, SAM-e,

Omega-3, raw-food diets, gratitude diaries – or have we thought about therapy?

'Yep. It is shit.'

She asked me if it was hard to leave G behind.

'The kids keep him going somehow. My worry is what will happen when they're old enough to move on. I'm not sure I can do it on my own. I feel a bit lost, to be honest.'

Lights were placed on the bow that night, but even then, we couldn't see more than a few metres ahead. Klaas had warned us to look out for growlers – lumps of ice, *small as cars on the surface, big as trucks underneath* – as they didn't show up on the radar. Snow petrels flitted in the bright lights like moths. We did our best to see past them, keeping a keen watch, but the wind stung our faces and shrilled through the rigging. I felt relieved to crawl into my bunk at the end of our shift that night.

The following day, our twelfth at sea, we watched the afternoon squalls race across the sky as South Georgia rent the horizon, rising like rotten dog's teeth from the sea. White glaciers sloughed off its sides, dark where ice had scoured its way to the black bone. The weather had not yet had its fill of us, and a fierce squall hit as we battled to bring in the floundering sails. The waves, from all directions, slapped their crests together, casting arcs of spray high into the air.

As we approached the island, the scent of seaweed wafted over us. It took me back to childhood day-trips to the beach – *I can smell the sea,* I'd shout as we neared the coast. But now, after so long away from land, I realised the smell was not the sea, but the shore.

After two hours, we closed the distance and sailed into the sudden calm of Rosita Harbour. The anchor dropped into the still waters of the bay, and the sound of barking seals echoed from the shore.

~

The *Southern Venturer* sails from Newcastle on 27 October 1948, and it's an early start to catch the tide. A few of the whale men's wives stand on the dock and give a nod to their husbands. A fellow whale ship sounds a single toot on the ship's whistle, then four straining tug-boats tow the *Southern Venturer* out of port. She wallows top-heavy, the oil tanks in her hull empty, the deck laden with supplies. Though your head is a little groggy, you're already up, making strong coffee for the men. You're faring better than the others, who nurse delicate heads and stomachs with aspirin and slices of dry bread. It feels good to be busy, and your worries of last night have eased as you get stuck into the job. Though the men at your tables are demanding, they are kind too and treat you well. You like to listen to their chat, learning about the different jobs they do.

Two days later, the ship anchors in Tønsberg fjord, Norway, to pick up the rest of the crew for the journey south. Tønsberg is prosperous, smartly built and painted, courtesy of supplies pilfered from all the whale ships that have docked here over the years, so rumour has it. The town even smells of whale, most of the houses scrubbed clean with soap made from whale oil. You don't bother to go ashore. Danny tells you everything is too expensive here.

As there is no dock or wharf in Tønsberg large enough for the ship, the cargo and Norwegian crew are ferried out on motorboats. You help to load bags and boxes: crates of tinned meat and dried fish stiff as shoe-leather alongside bundles of colourful wool sweaters, rubber boots, oilskins and boxes and boxes of coffee. The Norwegian crew boards, carrying a fine array of guitars and mandolins, their bags clinking with bottles. They greet the other men with back-slapping hugs. They all have canvas wash buckets too – even the expedition manager, who has a three-room suite and a bathroom of his own. The flensers, the men who slice the blubber from the whales, carry hockey-stick knives wrapped in sackcloth. The Norwegians are blond and weather-beaten but smart and well dressed.

The gunners, the men who captain the catcher boats and fire the harpoons, are on strike, unhappy with their pay, though they are rumoured to get £4,000 a trip, plus an extra £30 for each whale shot. It seems a fortune. They are wealthy men, treated like celebrities in Tønsberg, the gateways to their houses marked by great arches of whale bone. The success of the fleet depends on them.

You hear the top gunner last year was Arne Mikalsen. The catcher boat crews are paid based on a share of the catch, and Danny is desperate to be assigned to Arne's crew.

The gunners refuse to board, but the ship sails anyway, chased by a flotilla of boats sounding their horns and full of women wretched at the sight of their husbands and sons departing. You watch as the men hang over the rails waving back, thinking of how the ship left Newcastle with barely a handful of people to say their goodbyes from the dock.

Twelve miles out, and queues form along the deck to the slop-chest, the ship's store. Once in international waters, all goods are duty-free, so the men get in line to stock up on cigarettes. Everything you might need for the season is sold here, though no alcohol.

You queue with Danny to get yourself a new jacket – one of the short woollen ones like most of the other lads wear.

Danny tells you that you'd do well to learn Norwegian, and when your turn comes, you buy a teach-yourself-Norwegian book and a dictionary along with your new jacket. No money is exchanged, and some of the new men go mad with it, thinking everything is as good as free, but you're careful, knowing the cost will be deducted from your wages.

You're kept busy with the other boys working in the whalers' mess feeding around 350 men, three times every day, plus coffee and biscuits mid-morning and afternoon. Eight a.m. breakfast, midday lunch and evening supper at six. You have a table of twenty to look after. The other lads in your cabin work in the artificers' mess feeding the Group I whalers: the bosuns, chief flensers, head winch-men and deck bosses. They are more exacting in their standards and expect the place to be kept spotless, their meals served on time, but the pay is better.

The highest pay for mess boys is earned in the officers' mess. The chief steward sends you along there with new crockery one day, and you recognise Ferguson, the manager you met at your medical. He calls you over and asks how you're getting on.

'If you keep your head down and work hard, you'll get moved up to the artificers' mess and maybe even up here,' he tells you. 'More money,' he says rubbing his fingers together. You feel pleased he's remembered you. The officers' mess is quiet and clean, just a few small tables to wait on. You decide to work your way up the ladder as fast as you can.

Soon lists appear on the noticeboards, detailing the work gangs. There is a strict hierarchy among the whalers. Many of the Group I whalers – the head flensers and lemmers – will not work until whaling begins, but the Group VIII whalers, the unskilled men from your mess, are tasked with the worst jobs. There is plenty to do to ready the ship for her season. Large squads sit out on deck splicing whale lines. The carpenters direct the laying of a new pine deck; each year a fresh one is laid over the ship's teak deck and then dumped overboard, bloodied and battered at the end of the season. The noise of the engine is overwhelmed by the constant buzz of electric saws until the finished deck is as smooth as Formica, with perfectly fitting circular hatches covering the boiler openings.

The blacksmiths busy themselves making harpoons. Other men dangle from ropes over the ship's side, repainting the hull.

The job you hate the most is down in the ship's stores sorting the crates of potatoes stashed in every spare nook and cranny on board the ship. They must be regularly tipped out, turned over and any rotten ones thrown away. The worst are eggshell-thin, green and liquid inside. They burst easily to release their foul-smelling contents, compounding any seasickness in those suffering, though you've a hardier stomach. Many men cheat, just turning over a few potatoes at the top of the crate, but though you hate the job you make sure it's done properly.

The galley is well equipped, with huge oil-burning ranges and an electric bakery. There are chief cooks of both nationalities, and the menu alternates between British and Norwegian dishes. The food is good and plentiful. You relish the abundance, eating your way through half a pound of cheese a day, as well as eggs, beef and unlimited supplies of vegetables and fruit.

Thirty live pigs are kept aboard, tended to by Tam, the pigman. The other mess boys hate taking the slops out to them, but you always volunteer. You like the way they run up to greet you, squealing. There's one that's your favourite. He's a little smaller than the rest. He hangs at the back, but you always make sure to save him the best slops and leave him a pile of his own away from the other pigs as they fight at the trough. He lets you scratch his rough and spotted hairy back as he eats. You nickname him Pork Scratchings.

When you take the slops out, you and Tam often stand leaning on the makeshift fence to watch them and talk about the different personalities they all have. Pork Scratchings is the shy one, Bully Boy always pushes to the front when there's food around. You've even named one Ferguson because he's huge and squeals the loudest. As the weather warms, you help Tam hose the pigs down to cool them off. They love it.

Working in the galley one day, the steward sends you to give Tam a hand. When you get down there, Pork Scratchings lies outside the pen with his throat slit ear to ear.

'Ah, Tony, give us a hand to hoist this fellow up to the galley. You've done a grand job fattening him up. He'll make a good Sunday roast for the men,' Tam says, chuckling. You thought the pigs were all bound for South Georgia. You hadn't realised that some would be killed on the journey. Pork Scratchings is hoisted by winch to the upper deck and then, like an injured soldier, stretchered into the galley. You and three other lads take a corner each.

That evening you lie in your bunk and open Aunt Lottie's bag of tablet, taken back to the warm smell of her kitchen. It's the first time since leaving Newcastle that you feel the piercing pain of homesickness.

The ship sails south at three and a half degrees a day. Off the coast of Morocco, you stand at the stern taking your afternoon break and watch white foam spiral off the twin screw propellers. The seas glint under the kind of sun that warms through to your bones. Last night, the heat in your cabin above the engines had become so stifling you dragged your rubber mattress out to sleep on deck and relish the cool night air, watching the stars, lulled by the gentle motion of the ship and the thrum of its engines.

Danny finds you. 'Come for a swim,' he says. 'The chippies have set up a canvas tank on the deck and filled it with seawater.' You tell him you'll come and watch. You can't swim, and though the pool is shallow enough to stand in, you can see from the boisterous games already being played that you wouldn't enjoy it.

Tenerife soon rises lush from cobalt seas, and the ship heads into port for fuel. Nobody seems to mind that most of the men get blind drunk in the dockside bars. It's usual. One of the crew got so drunk in Tønsberg that he missed the boat. You're not so keen on drink after your experience in the Jungle, so you decide to explore the streets of Tenerife on foot. The population is poor and desperate, and you are beset by hawkers and beggars, so you soon turn around and head back to the ship.

The gunners have ended their strike and are flown out to join you. The crew is complete and sails from Tenerife with 180 British and 300 Norwegians, plus three stowaways – two of them British sailors who boarded the wrong boat while drunk, and Manuel from Tenerife. The year before, twenty-three stowaways sneaked on, Danny says. Stowaways worked their first season for free but got paid a full wage after that. Manuel joins your table in the mess, happy to be on board. 'I will return to Tenerife a wealthy man if I stay over the winter,' he tells you.

As you cross the equator, a cabaret is held to celebrate. The Norwegians recite long dirgy songs, finding them funny, though you can't understand the words yet. Manuel stands and sings two plaintive Spanish ballads, his soulful voice spilling out across the sea. The men listen in rapt silence, exploding into applause as the last notes ebb into the balmy night. That pang of homesickness hits you in the gut once more.

Life on board is relaxed, though. There are few formalities and no dress code. Most of the men stop shaving at Tenerife. No need to look their best any more. The other new mess boys seem bold and confident, imagining themselves to be full-blown whale men already earning big bonuses, with scant idea of the graft ahead. You keep your head down, determined to get on well with your work. In the evenings in your mess, the Norwegian men play bridge, ebullient when they win.

'Why the hell didn't you play like a king?' they shout in Norwegian, throwing down their winning cards. You study your Norwegian books each evening and practise on the men, slowly picking up words here and there.

Some evenings, bingo is played on deck under floodlights, and sometimes five-a-side football too, though it's often cut short by injury and feels too rough for you.

In the black turbulence of the Roaring Forties, the first albatross skim the deck. You are mesmerised by the way they fly and how perilously close they come to hitting the bridge at times.

'Stash all the breakables away in the lockers,' the chief steward tells you one evening after supper. 'And make sure all the doors are latched tight. We've a rough few days ahead.'

Sure enough, that night a wretched storm blows up. Huge seas roll up the rear slipway of the ship and wash clear over the plan, flooding the lower decks. Pumps work full tilt to dry everything out, and you're set to work with a mop and bucket. In the galley, the best the chefs can rustle up are a few sandwiches each for the men – just as well, as you are short-handed, with so many of the mess boys lying curled up in their bunks with seasickness, including the two lads in your cabin. You feel proud of yourself for the hardiness of your stomach, and the chief steward tells you how well you're doing. You lurch around the mess room, imagining it must be easy to spot a sailor on land, unable to walk with their feet together.

After the excitement of the storm, your routine returns to normal. The days begin to drag; it's a slow journey south at twelve knots, and for each degree of increasing latitude, the temperature drops further, but you're kept busy laying out tables and clearing up afterwards. There's bickering with the other thirty or so mess boys to get into the washroom to clean the dishes and cutlery after meals, and now you join in the arguments about who takes out the slops to the pig pen – you're no longer keen to do so.

As the air cools, the activities on deck cease, and most of the men occupy themselves reading or playing chess. The atmosphere turns quiet, and a moodiness settles on the men.

'Nae women! And none in sight for another six months at least!' one of the whalers tells you.

'Every year, we all say it'll be our last, but every bloody year we come back,' another says.

Danny tells you it's just boredom and the men will cheer up when the ship reaches South Georgia, then more so on the killing of the first whale. Sure enough, as the island looms, the gloom lifts; singing is once again heard on board. You help to move stores and supplies into heaps on the deck, ready to be transferred to the catcher boats, a pile for each.

On 1 December, just over a month after setting out, you near Leith Harbour, South Georgia. The bitter weather descends, the southern summer already colder than a Scottish winter. You're in good health, your hair thickened and nails grown strong on plentiful food, ready for the season of work ahead.

3

Landfall

We explored the sheltered northeast coast of South Georgia
for several days, ferried ashore here and there for a closer
look. The wildlife – penguins, fur seals, elephant seals –
seemed indifferent to us, their lack of fear borne of having
no land predators, and though a two-metre rule kept us
away from them, they didn't obey it. We'd had our mandat-
ory lectures on the strict visitor protocols. Lex had provided
us with our Antarctic mantra – *leave nothing, take nothing,
not even a stone*. We'd vacuumed the pockets of our jackets
and picked fluff and grass seeds from our Velcro; we'd
cleaned and disinfected our boots, scoured every crevice of
tread: the introduction of alien species to this landscape
could be catastrophic. Although humans, it seemed, were
allowed.

South Georgia is a fleck of an island in the midst of the vast
Southern Ocean. At fifty-four degrees south, if you sailed
west from its shores, after 1,000 miles you'd land at Cape
Horn, the southernmost tip of South America. If you sailed
east instead, following the trade winds, you'd also land at
Cape Horn, though after a much longer journey. No other
land lies at this latitude.

In Fortuna Bay, mist drifted thin and low across the slick sea. A lone iceberg bobbed half stranded near the shore, bright against the dull rubbled land. We stepped ashore, carrying in our rucksacks the lunches we'd packed at break-fast – white bread only, nothing with seeds, no fruit – and stood in silence waiting for the fog to lift, listening to fur seals calling across the bay.

Lex, hands on hips, looked up to the peaks above us. 'Once the fog lifts, we'll do the last part of Shackleton's walk over the hill to Stromness.'

After the *Endurance* sank, Shackleton sailed to Elephant Island and dropped off most of his men before he continued on to South Georgia with a crew of five in a small leaky life-boat. Frozen and malnourished, they landed on the wrong side of the island; South Georgia has two very different faces. On the southwest coast, cliffs plunge into the sea, and on the sheltered northeast coast, the land levels more gently to natural harbours and inlets. The whaling stations lay on the northeast side. Taking Frank Worsley and Tom Crean with him after a few days' rest, and leaving the three weak-est men on the shore, Shackleton crossed the island on foot wearing sodden leather boots, screws driven through the soles for grip, carrying scant supplies and an old hessian rope. The men traversed the complex ground of glaciers and crevasses without crampons or ice axes in thirty-six hours. They had no map and only a pocket compass. In the year 2000, three experienced climbers retraced Shackleton's thirty-four-mile route. They were fit, well conditioned and had all the latest mountain equipment. It took them three days.

We were only following the final few miles of the walk. As we made our way up the sparsely tussocked slope, I stopped to catch my breath and look down at our ship, turning around her anchor, sails hoisted and rucked on her yards.

'Some view, isn't it?' said Kate, catching up with me.

I started to get my geologist's eye into the landscape, finding features I'd studied and taught but only ever seen in textbooks and photos. To our left, a gritty glacier slaked down the mountainside, seeping milky meltwater into the bay. Half a mile or so off its snout, a linear island marked its previous extent. I pointed it out to Kate. 'That's how much these glaciers have melted over the last twenty years or so. Utterly frightening to see it in reality.'

As we headed up to the high plateau, the grass and moss petered out to leave a landscape of slate, meticulously organised into stripes and circles by millennia of heaving frosts, as if Sisyphus himself, tired of pushing one of the giant boulders now strewn across the hillside, had decided to stop and tidy up a bit.

Towards the summit, on a flat plateau, nestled Crean Lake, where Tom Crean fell through thin ice and landed up to his waist in freezing water. Shackleton and Worsley hauled him out, and they carried on.

We crested the pass, and the view stretched away from us to Stromness whaling station on the shore of a broad sheltered harbour. Between us and our pick-up point lay scree: the entire vast valley was smothered in a post-apocalyptic stratum of rough unsorted rubble that flanked the slopes and filled the valley floor. It was split and sliced by meltwater channels, etched by streams and puddled by lakes. This is what ice leaves behind. It scrapes and grinds its way across landscapes, prises rocks apart, pulverising and shovelling through, leaving nothing but debris when it melts.

Years before, I'd worked with a team of academics recreating ancient landscapes in virtual reality. We interpreted rocks, landforms and tiny grains of pollen preserved in the soils, and pieced together rich pictures of places and how they'd evolved through time. We once made a film of Loch Lomond from 10,000 years ago as the last ice-sheets ebbed away from Scotland's shores. It looked exactly like this: a place scraped clean of everything but rock and rubble. Moving through time, the film showed the first simple lichens and mosses colonising the land, then tussock grass, the first shrubs and trees – birch, hazel, juniper, ash, Scots pine and oak – and finally, the most rapid and profound transformation of all: the arrival of humans. Felled forests and roads divided land into neat parcels, laced with cables. Over time, the warming of our climate would reshape this South Georgia landscape too, soothing the brittle earth into something different, something softer and green.

Looking out across Stromness Bay, a tiny dot moved slowly towards the harbour. Kate raised her binoculars. 'That's our ship. She looks so small from here. So insignificant.'

Shackleton, Worsely and Crean stood in this very spot and heard the station's whistle call the whalers to their morning's work. They saw movement and life, smoke rising from boilers, their first sight of other people after seventeen months of exile. I can only imagine the relief.

We slid our way down to the bay, crossing scree slopes and snow-filled hollows, and on the valley floor we followed the braided desire lines of the gentoo penguins which nested a mile inland. At the northern edge of the whaling station, upturned propellers drilled down into the pebbled beach; fur seals slept along their spiral curves and whale spines sleeked across the foreshore. In the early days of whaling, the whalers took only the blubber – the richest source of whale oil – and left the stripped carcasses to rot in the bay. Nowadays, in summer, the clear shallow waters along the shore fill with fur seal pups waiting for their mothers to return from the hunt.

The whaling station caught me by surprise. I knew little of the whaling history here, had not expected it. I'd known colleagues who'd travelled here before me to study the landscape, the glaciers, the wildlife. They'd returned with spectacular photos and stark warnings of climate change, but nothing of whaling. Or had I not been paying attention? Here it was, in its ugly truth: South Georgia, unmistakably, was once the central hub for this brutal industry. Now the island lay asset-stripped and looted, left only with the rusted remains of these old whaling stations.

A closer look at the shoreline revealed more bone than stone. An upturned vertebra lay sculpted, organic and aged, the size and shape of a coffee table, the colour and texture of driftwood, porous and smudged with a faint tint of algal green. I sat down on it, rubbed my hands across its roughened surface, trying to sense the life it once contained.

~

You can smell the whaling station before you see it, pungent as chloroform. Two years have now passed since you arrived here as a fresh-faced mess boy working your first season. The smell takes you back to the horror you felt that day, seeing the place for the first time. Even this time, your third season, it's still shocking: the mud, the mess, the discarded and rusty machinery piled under dirty heaps of snow. You'd imagined the Antarctica of the explorers' stories you'd read as a boy. South Georgia was nothing like that.

On your first trip, you kept your head down as Ferguson advised. You learned fast, and while the other lads messed about having water and HP Sauce fights, you got on with the job, and became near fluent in Norwegian too. It didn't make you popular, but neither did it go unnoticed by the chief steward. By your second season, you'd worked your way up to the artificers' mess, and this year, another promotion, to the officers' mess. You take pride in your job – your crockery gleaming and perfectly placed on the tables, plates of food served from the left and cleared from the right, sparkling crystal and polished silver. You take good care of your appearance too, always smart, your clothes clean and ironed. *Always look your best*, as your mum would say. It has been hard work and long hours, but worth it.

When you arrived home at the end of last season, your pockets full of money, the family gathered as you handed out presents: watches for Robbie and Gerry, a whale's tooth for Michael, a silver bracelet for Mary and musical jewellery boxes for your mum, Nana Lina and Aunt Lottie. You treated your dad to a pint at the local pub. 'I'm proud of you, son,' he said.

You saved the rest of your pay, careful to make it last over the summer, and took on odd jobs here and there until signing on again for a third season. Salvesen was pleased to have you back.

As the *Southern Venturer* sails into the calm waters of Leith Harbour, smoke surges from the boiler-house chimneys on the shore; the whaling season has begun here already, the flensing platform busy and bloodied from the first few catches of the year. The blubber boilers, meat and bone cookers billow steam into the crisp morning air. At the north end of the bay, a row of catcher boats are moored nose to shore in the shallow waters, the grey hulls and the red, white and blue funnels freshly painted.

As you dock at the small wharf, the overwinterers stand quayside, excited to see your ship after being cut off from the world for the last six months, eager for their mail and news from home, welcoming back old friends and supplies of fresh food, and best of all, the excitement of another season. You see Danny's familiar face on the dock and wave to him. He loves the winters here – you can't understand why, you've never much liked winters at home, let alone in this dark place. He looks lean and fit.

It takes a while to moor the ship. Arm-thick wire hawsers are fastened around bollards and ground anchors onshore. The catcher crews transfer to their boats, fire up belching engines and swarm the ship. The job of transferring equipment, food, fuel and water begins. Radars and radios are tested, harpoons tied onto nylon lines. The gunners bark orders at their crew. Before long, the catchers circle the bay, firing at floating targets, eager to get going.

Leith Harbour whaling station is huge: a ramshackle sprawl of eclectic buildings, most with white wooden sides and corrugated iron roofs like some Wild West town hastily thrown up in a gold rush. Snow is piled high where it's been endlessly shovelled over the winter into colossal heaps. The whaling station has everything for self-sufficiency. There is an abattoir and pigsty, though most of the pigs roam free among the elephant seals and penguins; the main thoroughfare is known as Pig Street. In the station centre are the workshops: the welding plant, the plumbers' shop, the engineering office, the carpenters' shop and the boiler cleaners' store. There is even a power station fuelled by coal brought in on the factory and supply ships.

You visit the station 'slop-chest,' the large three-storey building with a steep roof that houses the store. Here they sell almost everything: tea, tobacco, sugar, soap, toothpaste, jackets, watches, skis and boxes of Cadbury's chocolates. You can even send marconigrams, though they're expensive and generally kept for the exchange of news on births and deaths. You sign a docket for your goods – new boots so you can go walking and explore a little. Most things are pretty cheap, cheaper than you can buy at home, anyway.

The *Southern Venturer* stays in port for a week, and you're kept busy working in the galley – the men still need to eat – but after work, you walk the lower paths around the bay, making the most of the long light evenings, careful not to go too far.

The landscape is rocky, with little that's green except for mosses and tussock grass growing around the fringes of the shore, but the scenery is impressive, rivalling the Highland lochs of Scotland, not that you've ever seen them other than on calendars and in picture books. You look out for the reindeer, introduced to the island fifty years ago to provide food and sport for the whale men, but you don't see any. There are plenty of penguins, though, nesting close to the station and conveniently breeding at the start of the season so the men have a good supply of fresh eggs. There are rats too, huge brown rats. They send a shudder right through to your new boots.

On the voyage down here this year, on Ferguson's advice, you'd read *South*, Shackleton's account of his epic expedition, and on one of your evenings off, you walk over to the repair station at Stromness, keen to see the place where Shackleton ended his journey.

You follow the path south from Leith Harbour, out past the football pitch where the king penguins hang around when moulting. You climb the steep hill up to Hansen Point and stop on a sandbagged platform overlooking Stromness Bay to look at the rusted giant gun pointing outwards to the harbour entrance, installed during the war to defend the station in the event of an invasion. The gun is guarded now by a lone fur seal bull. He bares his teeth at you in a half-hearted sneer as you skirt wide around him. Seal bites are notorious for becoming infected; you've seen more than one whaler with a badly swollen hand from the dreaded 'seal finger' infection.

Stromness is in the same ramshackle state as Leith Harbour, but as it's just a repair station, there isn't the soup of stinking whale intestines rotting in the bay. You can see up to the cliff where Shackleton and his men would have stood looking down at Stromness for the first time. You can't imagine how they felt, lost and stranded like that for seventeen months.

You tell Ferguson about your walk the next morning as you clear away the breakfast dishes.

'Sit,' he says. 'Let me tell you. I was here the day Shackleton walked in from the mountains. I was in the manager's office at Stromness. Everybody there knew Shackleton well. Cautious Jack, we called him. Funny, really, when you think about it. But we did not know the terrible-looking bearded men who walked in from the mountain that morning. "Well? Who are you?" the manager asked. The man in the centre of the three said, "Don't you know me? My name is Shackleton," and then he asked when the war had finished, but the war was still on.'

Ferguson sits in silence for a while, looking down at the floor.

The following evening, the island's magistrate boards the ship to dine in the officers' mess at Ferguson's invitation.

Robertson, the factory-ship doctor, is there too. You stay behind late into the evening to wait on the men, topping up their whiskies and lighting their cigars.

The men discuss conditions at the whaling station. Ferguson took the men on a tour there earlier, and Robertson was shocked.

'I've travelled to Glasgow, Cairo, Calcutta and Shanghai, and I can tell you, Leith Harbour is the most sordid habitation of men I've ever seen,' Robertson begins, warming up his rage. 'What commercial greed can do at the expense of human dignity is nauseating.' He slams down his whisky glass on the table, spilling a little. You step forward from the corner, wipe the table and refill his glass.

Sinclair, the factory's whaling inspector, weighs in on the discussion. 'You're right, Robertson.' He points through the window to the Union Jack flying over the station manager's house on the shore. 'I'm ashamed to see our flag flying over this dung-heap.'

You notice Ferguson's face fall. He took the men on a tour to show off the facilities. Robertson turns to him, adding, 'The machinery is in beautiful order, of course. But it's the waste, that's the problem – the whale parts that aren't used and just dumped into the harbour to rot. The men live amongst this filth year-round. The only decent place here is the manager's house.'

Robertson is right. You've seen the conditions for yourself: the paths thick with mud, the barracks filthy, and the all-pervading stench of decay enveloping the station like a thick fog.

'It's clear from the books the men read,' Robertson continues, 'the photographs they take, the way they talk about the rest of the island, that these whalers appreciate the beauty of things, and yet this is how they live? There is no bar, no canteen, no clubroom, church or garden. Well, there is the kino of course, but it's just a dirty hut, hardly a cinema – and only five films for the entire year! And as for the so-called hospital, don't get me started.' He slams down his glass again.

He'd not even seen the worst of it, you think. In your second season, as the fleet was in port preparing to head south, you'd been roped in to help out a new doctor. He'd arrived to find the 'hospital' was only eight beds in a hut – for 600 men. He'd begged and pilfered materials and, with help from convalescing patients, upgraded it to a smarter fourteen-bed unit. But still, it couldn't be called a hospital, and the doctor had to do every manner of operation himself with only an untrained mess boy to help. Badly injured men could lie for many months until they travelled home on one of the supply ships. Though the doctor often asks for injured men to be shipped to Montevideo and flown home for specialist treatment, the whaling company never agrees to it; the men are not worth the time and money it would take to get them home. Even during the war, injured men were evacuated to a proper hospital within four days of injury, but at Leith Harbour, they could lie for up to a year without proper treatment.

'Is there nothing the British Government can do to enforce better conditions for the men?' Robertson asks, turning to the magistrate.

The magistrate breathes a heavy sigh. He says that whaling keeps the British people in margarine and soap. 'I'll tell you a story about this,' he says. 'A few years ago, a transport vessel belonging to a British whaling company asked for clearance to sail home with 400 men on board. I denied permission on the basis that they had no doctor and were carrying some very sick men.' He explains how the whaling company contacted the Ministry of Food, telling them there would be no margarine that year as their ship had been held up by a petty official on a triviality. 'I received a cable from the Prime Minister's office twelve hours later telling me to release the ship immediately.' The whisky has loosened the magistrate's tongue. 'I have less power than a flenser over these whaling companies.'

Ferguson, unusually quiet until now, speaks up, unable to contain his anger. 'And what do we do it all for, eh? We go down to the ice year after year, live in stink and filth. Some of us don't even make it back. The company doesn't care about us. We're just here to make them rich.'

When the men finally retire, you clear away their glasses and sweep their anger from the table. But you begin to feel a rage rise in your own chest too. Like most of the whalers, you've never questioned the working conditions before.

~

At anchor in Leith Harbour, Kate and I sat out on the bow deck, looking towards the whaling station. The day was overcast, and a light mist skimmed the bay. Lex appeared, offering us a trip in the Zodiac to take a closer look at the station, and we rushed to our cabin to pull on waterproofs and grab cameras. Back out with our gear, we climbed down the rope ladder dangling over the rails and into the waiting boat.

'I like the hat,' said Lex as I took the seat next to him.

I'd put on my Sea Shepherd beanie with its skull and cross-bones logo. It seemed appropriate.

Lex pushed off from the ship and steered towards the shore.

Kate asked me about Sea Shepherd. I told her about Paul Watson, who set up the organisation in the 1970s. He was a man I'd always found intriguing. Compassionate but ruthless, I thought of him as Kurtz – not the sickly man in Conrad's *Heart of Darkness*, but Marlon Brando's corpulent Kurtz in Coppola's *Apocalypse Now*. This was Watson: a charismatic renegade flanked by rebel soldiers, a warrior poet. He had gone rogue on Greenpeace, which he helped to found, after being ousted for employing extreme direct action. His genius in harnessing media attention, in garnering multi-million dollar sponsorship, was unrivalled.

I first learned of Sea Shepherd through Animal Planet's series *Whale Wars*, which followed the group as they sailed to Antarctica in an old converted Norwegian catcher boat, chasing down the *Nisshin Maru*, a Japanese whaler factory ship, and blocking the transfer of whales from the harpoon boats to the factory's rear slipway using Zodiacs. Watson gently goaded his crew into ever more radical action, and the young, inexperienced volunteers often put themselves in harm's way. When criticised for not having a professional crew, Watson quoted Shackleton: 'I need men of passion, not professionals.' This teddy-bear-shaped man had a gravitas that could only come from complete conviction. I couldn't imagine having such certainty.

'Do they still hunt whales here?' Kate had to shout over the noise of the wind and the engine now.

'Yes,' I called back. 'The Japanese kill minkes and fins here every year. They say it's for research, but go into any market in Japan and you'll find whale meat.'

Leith Harbour whaling station lay heaped on the tideline like a wrack of seaweed. Grey-sided, red-roofed buildings flanked the shore, crumbling and stripped of their cladding by gales. We saw knotted machinery piled high. Sloughed in heaps alongside the rotten pier lay rusted engines, giant chains, barrels and ship propellers like felled windmills. The wreck of a catcher boat sat careened on the beach, a metal barrel topping the mast for lookouts hunkered down on cold shifts, watching for tell-tale blows. These sleek vessels, high at the bow where the gun is fixed toothpick-sharp, barbed and ready to snare, chased the whales to exhaustion before shooting them with explosive harpoons. We circled back to get a better look at the slipway, where winches heaved each groaning carcass onto shore for flensing, dicing and sawing, rendering into oil, fat, meal and meat. The world's most astonishing creatures reduced to lifeless barrelled commodities.

'Why has it been left in such a mess?' I asked Lex.

'Well, they were going to clear it up, but this is how your Falklands War began.' Lex idled the engine and we drifted. He cast his eye along the shoreline.

Christian Salvesen, the company that owned Leith Harbour, sold the scrap metal rights to an Argentine businessman. When his ship landed at Leith Harbour in March 1982, it was reported that they had raised the Argentinian flag. Royal Marines were dispatched from the Falklands to investigate and detained the workers. In response, Argentina sent troops to rescue them and invaded the Falkland Islands at the same time. Later on, Salvesen was bought out by a larger company, which was bought out by a bigger one still. So who is responsible?

Lex steered us towards a small crescent beach south of the whaling station and nudged the Zodiac onto shore. 'We can walk up from here a little way and take a closer look – it's outside the restricted zone.'

The air, pungent with the smell of fur seals, clung heavy around us. Clambering on to the narrow strip of shingle, we found our way blocked by an irate bull seal, nose in the air, his upper lip twitching into an Elvis snarl. He stood a good deal taller than me, propped up on bracketed flippers, turning his head side to side to size us up, his bravado undermined by plaintive intakes of breath – like someone startled over and over. *Huh, huh, huh.*

'If he charges, stand your ground,' said Lex. 'They usually stop.' Lex was as tall as the seal and armed with the Zodiac paddle, so I let him stand his ground and stood behind him. The seal lunged, puffed up and inflated with rage, disturbing a nearby rival. In the confusion, we slipped past and climbed up to the flat grassy plain behind the beach.

The fur seals were another of the island's success stories. Before the whalers came the sealers, who took fur seals for their pelts and elephant seals for their blubber. The sealers would beat them around their heads until, confused and panicked, they would bolt for the sea, where they could be butchered more easily once shot. The seals were all but wiped out when whaling began. But then, gradually, as a result of less competition with whales for food, the population grew, and the seals now fringed the South Georgia coastline in staggering numbers, fuelling the species' recovery throughout the Antarctic region.

A slant of weak sunlight fell on our faces. Rimmed by peaks rising steep from the sea, the whaling station sat at the base of a deep bowl; only the midsummer sun warmed this ground. Between the crags flashed tight patches of snow. Scree flanked the lower slopes where ice had locked hard around the rocks and flung grit and dirt down the mountainside. This was a place that could engulf you, swallow you whole, the outside world redacted into slivers of sky.

We walked up along the southern edge of the station, flat grey slates slipping beneath our feet. Yellow signs warned of asbestos and kept us out far better than any fence could. We followed the trickle of a glacial stream inland.

Lex stopped near a narrow footbridge over the stream to point out the storage tanks. 'They used whale oil for so many things. First for lighting, then later for margarine, soap and cosmetics, and to make glycerine for bombs. But cheaper alternatives always came along. The whaling companies had to come up with more inventive ways to use it.' I thought about the times I'd sat at my granny's dressing table as a child, smearing her lipstick – most likely made with whale oil – across my face. It was still in margarine then too. I'd have spread it on my toast, no doubt.

'When did it close?' I asked.

'1961. By that time there were hardly any whales left. They estimate nearly 2 million whales were killed here in the Antarctic.'

I couldn't imagine what seas filled with that many whales would even look like. We'd seen none on our journey here and none in the waters around South Georgia. The International Whaling Commission imposed quotas, but they weren't strict enough, and by the 1960s, the remaining whales were not worth the cost of catching. Economics stopped whaling rather than any thought for conservation. A Japanese company leased the station from Salvesen in the mid 1960s, but only for the quota. They used factory ships instead, catching whales that fed further south.

The rich oceanic ecosystem I'd imagined Antarctica to be was really only an impoverished and plundered version of its glorious original self, like an overgrown and scrubby carpark where rich woodland once stood. And yet the damage is virtually invisible. On the surface, the sea still looks wild and pristine; we don't see the emptiness below the waves. Wildlife documentary-makers work harder and harder, look in ever more obscure places to show us their version of untouched wilderness, but the truth is, there are barely even pockets of it left. Meanwhile, we're glued to our televisions in awe, imagining little is amiss.

How could people do this? And for what? Pet food, fertiliser? Things used up long ago, and nothing now to show for it. I felt the anger rising in me. I stomped off, hating the world, hating the people who had done this.

And that's when it happened. That's when the small unfussy graveyard caught my eye, tucked away on its own, hemmed by a neat white fence and shallow ditch to keep out the seals. A huddle of moulting penguins, glum as mourners, skulked nearby.

In my local churchyard, the headstones face towards the summit of the hill that stands over our village like a sentinel. *I will lift up mine eyes to the hills, from whence cometh my help* – the lines from my school psalm still run through me like a vein of quartz. But here, the graves faced out to the short glimpse of horizon beyond the harbour. Little chance that help might cometh here.

I pulled my jacket tighter around me. It was nearly midsummer but colder than a bleak January day at Leith Docks on the Edinburgh shore. My rage began to subside as I drifted along the neat lines of graves. Most of the headstones were white painted concrete, though a few dark imported monoliths bore Norwegian inscriptions and names: *Hansen, Kristiansen, Thorsen, Johansen, Svendsen, Halvorsen, Jørgensen, Larsen.* All sons. A few names sounded more familiar, inscriptions I understood: *Alexander MacNair, Bonesawman, Age 28; James Hutchison, Leith, Age 59; James Westwood, Age 29, Alloa.* And just one pale grey granite tablet, shipped in at great expense by the grieving family, no doubt: *In loving memory of my dear husband Andrew Williamson.*

Kate, on the other side of the graveyard, began whistling the theme tune to Laurel and Hardy as a penguin waddled towards us.

'Penguins are not funny,' Lex shouted. 'I hate it when wildlife films play silly music when they show penguins.' Kate and I giggled, despite Lex's irritation. As if to prove a point, the penguin paused, seemed to forget where it was going and turned on its fat triangular feet.

I returned my attention to the graves, and there it was, near the end of the last row, the small square of slate fixed to a simple white cross.

DECK GALLEY BOY

ANTONY FORD

EDINBURGH

DIED 20-4-1952

19 YEARS

It took the breath from me. So young, and from so near to where I lived. The image of my own son at home, caring, sensitive and shy, fell into focus. This boy was barely older.

I bent and brushed the moss from the plaque and read the inscription again. I thought about what a deck galley boy might have done. Perhaps on one of the catcher boats or factory ships. Died 20-4-1952. April. The start of winter here, bone-chillingly cold: the darkness, seven winter months ahead, a season of work after that. Another year away from home. No, I couldn't think about that.

I stood and took in the breadth of the place, the thin, scant scatteredness of it all. This huge bay, this small abandoned graveyard.

As we headed back to the beach, past the old football pitch with its battered and twisted goalposts, I began to imagine the games those young men might have played here, some relief to their blood-filled days, no doubt, but now only the fur seals kept goal.

Like a thick haar, melancholy draped over us as we motored back to the ship. Even Kate was unusually quiet. In the teal waters of the bay, a fur seal lolled, wrapped in a boa of bronze kelp. I imagined the slow life of seals, soft muffled bubbles rising around their ears, the lush kelp forests blown by a viscous wind of water, sheltering pups playing hide-and-seek among the long fronds, and whale bones laid to rest on the ocean floor, an anchor for new life. The deep water seemed so peaceful, so faraway – a slow-motion world where flensing knives and bonesaws didn't exist.

I felt so pierced by Anthony's grave; the image of it had lodged under my skin. Of all the names on the headstones, only his had snagged me. I'd imagined the whalers as hardy men with little compassion, killing and slaughtering their way through dwindling communities of every kind of whale. But then, there he was. A teenager. How on earth had he ended up in the thin soil of this place?

I'd come here in search of heroics, spectacle, the adventure-book version of Antarctica, the Attenborough scenes of teeming wildlife. I hadn't expected this dispiriting scrapyard.

*

We sailed over to Grytviken the following day to visit Shackleton's grave. The crew ferried us ashore, dropping us about half a mile along the peninsula. The graveyard sat away from the cluster of more modern buildings and the Grytviken whaling station. At the back, a roughly hewn and slender granite monolith stood at the head of Shackleton's grave.

Shackleton died of a heart attack in South Georgia the evening before his expedition to circumnavigate Antarctica. They laid him to rest on the island that ended his most epic adventure. To the grave's right lay a small square of granite, a monument to Frank Wild, his second-in-command, whose ashes were brought here to join him in 2011. During the austral summer, the graveyard fills daily with cruise-ship guests, identically kitted out in smart red sailing gear, who stand at Shackleton's graveside and toast his memory with a shot of Jameson whiskey. We were no exception, though more eclectic in our diverse attire. Our crew handed out small shot glasses and filled them to the brim. We raised our glasses to 'The Boss', then turned to toast Frank Wild too. G would have loved this. He was a huge Shackleton fan as well. I felt sad not to be able to share this moment with him.

So here it was, the pinnacle of my trip. I savoured the thin burning of whiskey seeping around my gums, and as tears welled up in my eyes, the image of that simple grave in Leith Harbour returned to me. Shackleton's story is the perfect and unexpected tale of daring, survival and hope. But for every Shackleton, there were thousands of Anthony Fords. And who raises a glass at their gravesides, these men whose aching backs laid the foundations for exploration, empires and the economic elite? Who mourns them? The whalers robbed our generation of the huge pods of blue whales, fin whales and humpbacks that had once filled these waters and were now almost emptied of them. Yet I couldn't help feeling the ache of young Anthony Ford's death and a rising wave of compassion towards the men that lost their lives here, abandoned in the graveyards scattered around this island, places few would ever visit.

On the front of Shackleton's gravestone was a shining star with his name underneath and on the back, a quote from Robert Browning: *I hold that a man must strive to the uttermost for his life's set prize.*

Why must we strive always? Man or woman. Where the fuck does *striving* ever get us? What drives our need to explore when perhaps the most important things are on our doorstep? Exploration is expansionist. It's about elbowing and nudging everything else aside, gradually clawing into newer and newer spaces. Without our expansionist obsession, there would still be whales here. But without polar research, we wouldn't have known about the leaky ozone layer. Without ice-core science, we would know far less about human impacts on climate change. We would be more oblivious of the fact that our spherical Earth really does have edges – thresholds over which we can irreversibly tip.

'That was so moving.' Kate came up behind me, looking over my shoulder at the gravestone. I couldn't find the words to reply.

On the path over to the shop and museum, thrust onto the shore, sat the *Petrel* – a catcher boat, harpoon gun still attached, her barrel empty of lookouts. She had sleek lines like a child's warship toy, the grey and red rust of her hull blending into the layers of rock in the mountains behind. I imagined the fat funnel from her midships belching fumes as she sped after her prey. When the supply ships rolled in to Grytviken, they brought fuel oil to power these killer boats.

The tanks were rinsed through – the slick discharged into the sea – and refilled with whale oil for shipping back home. Oil for oil.

Grytviken was the first populated place we'd set foot in for three weeks. It felt weirdly commercial, with a shop, post office, museum and even public toilets. Though only our ship was in that day, a queue had formed in the shop. I picked up some postcards for the family: a picture of penguins for my daughter, a leopard seal for my son and one of Frank Wild for G. On it I wrote, *To my right-hand man, thank you for holding the fort!*

I bought South Georgia stamps, priced in sterling, the familiar silhouette of the queen in the top-left corner, and posted the cards in the red letterbox outside. I nipped in to use the loo, drawn by the thought of a toilet that didn't move. Kate was at the sinks washing her hands. 'Have you seen these?' She held up one of the solid white bars of soap, stamped with 'EIIR' and a crown. 'Just in case anyone's in any doubt about who these islands belong to.'

Sarah Lurcock, director of the South Georgia Heritage Trust, gave us a tour of Grytviken whaling station, built in 1904 by Carl Anton Larsen, a Norwegian explorer working for the Compañía Argentina de Pesca. I felt overwhelmed by the whaling talk, the meat plants, the steam saws, the facts and figures. I couldn't think any more about the extermination of whales.

I left the tour and walked up to the small Lutheran church at the foot of the mountains behind the town. Steeply roofed in grey and spired like a gnome's hat, the fresh white walls and arched windows seemed oddly perfect against the backdrop of the wrecked whaling station. Inside, the church was light and airy with pale cream wood-panelled walls and pine pews lined up to face the altar. The unstirred air smelled a little musty. It took me back to my village church as a child, not as light and bright as this, but the same smell. Every week I went alone to the Sunday service. I'm not sure I believed in God – my family didn't – but I'd been drawn by the lull of ritual and repetition, the hush and reverence.

I looked through the arched windows to the mountain views outside and shuffled into a pew, sitting down on the creaky bench to enjoy the stillness. I wondered at all the prayers whispered in these pews, all the faithful voices raised in song in the hope of warding off the dangers these men faced on a daily basis. *To those in peril on the sea.*

I stayed lost in thought until the church door burst open. Peter strode in. 'Isn't this fantastic?' he beamed, gesturing around the simple space.

'It's beautiful, isn't it? How was your tour?'

'So interesting.' His brow furrowed. 'But I had no idea how many whales they killed.' He stood silent for a minute, taking in the church. 'I'm going up to ring the church bell.' He pointed to the stairs leading to an upper gallery. 'They said we were allowed to. I won't be disturbing you if I do?'

'Not at all. It would be lovely to hear the bell.'

I got up and wandered over to the far corner of the church where a wooden door led through to a small annexe housing the library. Pale daylight flooded through the windows onto books still laid out on tables, books neatly stacked on floor-to-ceiling shelves, small white borrowing cards in their wooden box on the desk, names scribbled in pencil. It felt like I'd stepped back in time to the 1970s. The rooms of my first school were large and airy like this and full of pale green calm, quiet footsteps on wooden floors, whispers in corridors, the kindness of nuns who would bend to hug me so tight I'd lose my breath in the dark folds of their habits. Life felt so uncomplicated back then. I had thought Antarctica would be like that too, that I could disappear into the folds of its simplicity. But even here, life felt conflicted and difficult. My Christian education had encouraged binary thinking: I was brought up to believe in right and wrong. There was no nuance to it, no guidance on navigating the greyscale of life. The slaughter of whales here was so wholly wrong, but were the men who killed them wrong? Was young Anthony Ford wrong? Did he know what he was doing? I had no certainty that I wouldn't have done the same in his shoes.

As I picked up a book from the table, turning it over in my hands, the bell began to ring out a clear toll.

~

The *Southern Venturer* is loaded with fuel and supplies, ready to sail south and begin the whaling season. A football match between the shore-based men and the pelagic whalers is held, fuelling more competitiveness than an Old Firm game in Glasgow. The rowdy spectators are joined by a group of gentoo penguins who apparently, Danny tells you, always turn up for matches. The shoremen win as usual – they've had more practice.

Before the ship leaves port, a few of the whale men walk over the narrow wooden bridge south of the station and across the stream to the small graveyard. They tidy up the graves and pay their respects to the men, some of whom they once knew and worked alongside.

Finally the lines are cast off; the *Southern Venturer* backs away from her moorings and edges out of the harbour flanked by an attentive flock of two buoy boats, two corvettes and thirteen catchers – one of the catchers left the day before to scout for whales in advance. The fleet is laden with everything it needs for the next three months, no matter what the Southern Ocean throws at it. At dinner, you notice Robertson's frown; he is beginning to feel the weight of responsibility for the 650 men in his care. Whatever serious accidents occur, and they will, he'll have to deal with them, often with the ship rolling in heavy seas beneath him.

You're busy in the galley, helping to prepare meals for the men, already sinking into the relentless drudgery of the whaling season.

The fleet heads south.

~

As our ship sailed from South Georgia along the coast, I leaned on the stern rails and thought about Shackleton's *Endurance*, its ghost sails luffing in the slow currents, deep in the indigo depths of the air-clear Weddell Sea. That moment, when their ship was crushed, the moment it lost its seaworthiness, was the turning point for Shackleton, the moment his mission changed from one of exploration to one of rescue and return, the moment he vowed to make sure every one of his men made it home alive. His men were lucky to be so valued. The whale men were not so lucky. Anthony was not so lucky.

I looked out towards South Georgia's coastline, hopeful of seeing a tell-tale whale spout or two. The glossy sea carried a long slow swell, and the engine throbbed beneath my feet, driving the boat in the absence of a breeze. The calm waters made for perfect whale-spotting weather. After visiting South

Georgia in 1902, Carl Anton Larsen reported sighting thousands of whales as they surrounded his ship in curiosity. Lex joined me at the rail. 'Do you see many whales here?' I asked.

'Rarely,' he replied. He let out a long sigh as he scanned the horizon. 'Whales are slow to recover and even slower to forget.'

Our watch system began again that night. 'What's our heading, Captain?' I asked as I took my turn at the helm.

Klaas raised his outstretched palm to the bow of the ship. 'South,' he said. 'We're heading due south.'

Part Two

BLUE

A map of the Southern Ocean will show you a cloth of blue, featureless as a paint swatch. But the map is not the territory – there is a depth to it, a slab, a hunk, a chunk of descending blue that would make minute our fields and mountains. The ocean has a dimension of its own. And it is the realm of the whale – a creature larger than any other to have roamed this planet. And our tiny ships but skim the surface. This plimsoll-thin line is the only point at which we meet, where our worlds collide, and this (that we should meet at all) is the whale's downfall.

4

Into the Blue

We were back sailing the ill-tempered and gnarly Scotia Sea, back to our living space heeled over at twenty-five degrees, back to bracing against the bathroom walls, soaping one-handed in the shower. The waves, in all directions, cascaded foam and soak across the decks. We rode each crest and trough; the decks fell away beneath us as we bounced into freezing dark spray. Wind-flung snow felt like grit in our faces and seeped into every gap of our heavy-weather sailing gear. My belly, once again, churned itself to knots.

Below us, the Scotia Sea, named after the ship used for the Scottish National Antarctic Expedition of 1902 to 1904, washes above an active tectonic plate, pockmarked by volcanoes and bounded by regular earthquakes, its outline defined by what lies beneath it: an underwater ridge shaped like an elongated horseshoe trailing from the tip of Tierra del Fuego, running eastwards through South Georgia, through the curve of the South Sandwich Islands then looping back westwards to meet the tip of the Antarctic Peninsula. Broken from shelves fringing the Weddell Sea, slabs of ice, miles long, run aground on the ridge, where they are cleaved into chunks by currents and set adrift into the Scotia Sea.

We resumed our watches. Large bergs showed on the radar, but growlers lay deep in troughs or against a backdrop of white spray on crests. A member of the permanent crew sat up the foremast as an extra pair of eyes, relaying the ice-state to the captain via a handheld radio.

On lookout just after midnight, harnessed to the rails that ran around the bow, I rode the waves as the ship bounced like a fairground ride. Heikki stood lookout on the other side, leaning into the wind, backlit by the green starboard light. He looked across to me, beaming.

'Are you happy?' he shouted.

'Yes,' I laughed.

'But are you happy deep down in your soul?' he shouted again, this time with a smirk, his grey hair a little longer now, straggling around his face in the wind.

And I *was* happy, mostly. I was happy to be back at sea, though I still felt the gnaw of all that that we'd seen in South Georgia. I had found my rhythm in the cyclic watch patterns and the space to hide away when I needed it, cooried down in a corner with a book or out on the stern watching the birds pivot in the wind. It was a free and expansive life, just the slow turning of each day over our patch of ocean.

The size of our world waxed and waned with the clarity of the air. I became obsessed with the horizon. On clear days, it sliced razor-thin, sapphire blue below the cut and baby-doll blue above. The world fell away at the edges, and we stared out beyond the curve into deep space. When squalls and storms drifted over, our world shrank, blurring its edges. Sometimes, citrus light threaded between sea and sky – good weather heading our way – and sometimes it darkened, roughened by colossal waves we could see from twelve miles out. Time to hoist the storm sails.

Parades and fanfares of seabirds circled our ship. I spent long spells watching them, in awe of the fecundity such a seemingly hostile habitat supported. The cape petrels, my favourite, soared on black and white speckled wings, hanging plump white underbellies, trailing tail feathers perfectly dipped into black at the ends. Favouring the backdrop of twilight, they wheeled in the evening sun, seeming more subtly shaded than their officially stark black and white and reminding me of home, when the January snow falls thick and low winter light casts a peachy glow across the tussock-speckled hills. They are known too as pintado – or painted – petrels, but their habit of pecking at the water for food also earned them the nickname cape pigeons, and they often follow ships for scraps thrown overboard – a legacy from the whaling days when factories sailed in a wake of blood.

I loved the snow petrels too, pure white with black beaks and beady eyes, about the same size and shape as cape petrels, with short stocky bodies and wingspans the length of my outstretched arm. They fluttered more, sometimes like swallows, especially at night in the bright bow light. The Antarctic prions were smaller, stouter and more delicate but terrific fliers, fast and erratic with twisting glides flashing the wide dark M that spanned their pale backs.

We'd left South Georgia on a close-haul; the wind hit us from the southwest, and the strong circumpolar currents pushed us further east, away from the South Orkney Islands, our intended destination. The wind backed and veered as depressions swept over us, and after two days of beating against storms we'd turned north again. 'If we can't get to where we want, we can at least have some good sailing in the meantime,' Klaas told us. On the third morning, warmer air and a steadier breeze fetched in from the west. The sun blistered off fresh seas. First mate Janke called our watch on deck. She stood tall, lithe, wide-footed and steady as a rock on the pitching deck as her sun-bleached hair whipped rag-tailed in the wind.

'We're going to wear the ship,' she said, a stub of chalk in her hand and a scale model of the ship balanced on the capstan cover in the centre of the deck. With the weather in our favour, we were to loop the stern of the ship through the wind so we could head southwest again. A quick and easy jibe in a yacht, on a tall ship with twenty-six sails to be handled, the manoeuvre took time. Janke chalked our intended loop onto the wooden deck and used the small model, complete with cloth sails and string ropes, to explain how we'd navigate the turn, each task carried out in a precise order.

We worked as a team, sometimes as many as six of us hauling a single rope. Janke guided us in clear command: *ease away, haul away, two-six-heave, hold, make fast*, never raising her voice beyond what was needed to be heard above the wind. If we struggled with the weight of the yards, Janke pitched in behind us and hauled with the strength of at least two, if not three, of us. 'It's just technique,' she laughed when we said as much. It took us well over an hour, plus another to tidy the tangle of ropes afterwards, coiling each neatly back on to its own worn wooden peg.

Among the permanent crew, the women equalled the men; they fed the soul of the ship, always first to go aloft in a storm, fierce and agile, their strength at odds with their size. Standing at a little over five feet, bosun Emma looked after everything from the decks up. Soft-faced, with searing blue eyes, she had the slow rolling walk of those more used to being at sea than on land. Even when the weather took a sudden turn and sails had to be stowed in haste, she exuded surety. When not aboard *Europa*, she skippered a refurbished Brixham trawler, taking out underprivileged kids for a sail-training charity. One of the three guides, Sarah Gerats, a visual artist immersing herself (often literally) in stark land-scapes, lived in Svalbard but regularly worked polar expeditions, both north and south. She had the radiant skin borne of high-latitude living and wore gorgeous hand-knitted Nordic sweaters. Each evening as we gathered for our meet-ing in the deckhouse, Sarah told us stories of Antarctic explorers, finding nuances and snippets to connect us to the history of these long-dead men.

Marianne and cook's mate Bear, who'd given up a good London career to join the *Europa* team, ran the galley. Even as the ship writhed in heavy seas, they'd turn out three full meals a day for sixty people, and they always baked a cake if it was somebody's birthday. Among the deckhands, Merle, Elsa, Natalie and Selene, fresh-faced young women, worked twelve-hour shifts without a single day off throughout the six-week voyage, not once moaning about the work or the cold, turning their hands to every job they were given. Cleaning the deckhouse at 3 a.m. one morning, Else told us with a grin, 'Sailing is what we love, cleaning is what we do.'

Our ship too was named for a woman – a Phoenician prin-cess and lover of Zeus in Greek mythology. The god turned himself into a sleek and handsome white bull to charm the young princess. She climbed on his back, and they fled to Crete, where Zeus made her queen. The bull gave his name to the constellation Taurus, and the princess gave hers to a continent. On our ship's bow, holding firm to the golden horns of a white bull's head, her long red hair trailing through the waves, rode the beautiful naked Europa.

At around fourteen years old, I'd sat in the career advis-
or's office at school, and she'd asked, with no attempt to
disguise the wearisomeness of her job, 'What do you want
to be?' Happier outdoors, my hands in mud and my feet in
wellies, I'd told the tweed-suited woman I wanted to be a
farmer. 'Oh no! You couldn't possibly be a farmer,' she said,
then paused before adding, 'You could be a farmer's wife,
perhaps.' I stopped short of asking how one might become a
farmer's wife, but I took her at her word and gave up my
dream of working the land and driving a tractor, though I
don't recall much disappointment. I wasn't ready to *be*
anything.

But I did spend the first half of my adult life in male-
dominated spaces, studying geology with only a handful of
women on the course, the tutors and lecturers all men, then
on to work as an academic in a science department, again
with few female colleagues. I never once had a female boss.

I was thrilled to see these *Europa* women doing what they
loved, being the role models I wanted for my daughter. It is
easy to fall into the footsteps of others, but they were stomp-
ing new paths in hefty boots. Early in the trip, while out on
the end of a yardarm in a steady breeze, the mainsail wrapped
around the rope I was standing on. I couldn't find my footing
to get back to the platform on the main mast. Stranded and
terrified, I looked down at the rolling sea far below. Selene,
still in her early twenties, made her way out to me, unwrapped
the sail and guided me back to the platform. Amongst these
fierce and competent women, I felt in safe hands. Klaas had
built a crew where capability, experience and work ethic
formed the basis of respect for those in the chain of command,
and though, as always on a ship, a strict hierarchy operated,
it never seemed so. The women slotted naturally into this

way of working: without differences, without confrontation, without ego.

After wearing the ship, our watch breezed into the deck-house, invigorated by graft and air. Everyone was in high spirits. It was the eve of Sinterklaas, the feast of St Nicolas celebrated on 6 December in most of Europe, and the ship smelled of cinnamon, nutmeg and cloves. Marianne clattered in with a basin of dough to roll into *pepernoten*, the tiny spicy biscuits thrown to children by Sinterklaas and his helper Piet. I sat with Kate between helm and lookout stints, my water-proofs rolled down to my knees while I warmed up, rolling the sticky dough into small balls and placing them in neat lines on a baking tray. Heikki plugged his phone into the music system and played a country version of 'You Are My Sunshine'. Kate and I sang along, swaying together, side by side. *Please don't take my sunshine away.*

'Always chokes me up, that song,' said Kate as the tune ebbed away.

I felt choked too. It was a song I'd always sung to my kids; my grandmother had sung it to me.

I'd not heard from home for days. The ship's email and Internet system had succumbed to a generic 'electrical fault', and the crew was gathering what information it could on ice conditions and weather via satellite phone, but it wasn't ideal. 'It just makes the planning a little more adventurous and interesting,' Klaas reassured us.

We were fifty-eight degrees south and nearing austral midsummer. I woke just before midnight for the dog watch, the smell of fresh bread seeping into our cabin. We slept clos-est to the galley, and the crew baked through the night, a fresh loaf always delivered to those on watch. I stepped out on deck to catch my bearings and let the cold pinch me awake.

The sea rolled in a long swell, and the sky glowed deep lilac around the edges. On our starboard side, a huge iceberg hung on the horizon, almost the colour of the sky, barely visible unless you squinted and looked just to the side of it, like trying to see a faint star. Our sails hung ruffled and listless. We chugged through the pale dawn, barely daring to chat, even in hushed tones, lest we broke the reverie. As the sky brightened, the berg glowed a little brighter. The shadow of a giant petrel crossed our port side, a single squawk puncturing the silence.

'Whale sprouts,' shouted Heikki, stood at the helm. I didn't correct him and later took to shouting the same whenever I saw a whale; I liked the idea of whales sprouting up from the sea. Misty columns rose and ebbed off our starboard side.

'Fin whales,' said Klaas, climbing the steps up from the bridge and looking through his binoculars. 'Second biggest whale after the blue. See the blow? Tall and narrow, like the blues, but not quite as high.'

Great slick black backs, ridged like upturned hulls, rolled from the double-nostril lumpen blowholes to the small, rudder-like dorsal fins, tails rarely showing. The whales swam some way off, but it looked like a small pod, rolling and breathing, rolling and breathing, like long sleek eels. Soon they overtook us and disappeared on the horizon. 'Greyhounds of the sea,' Klaas said, 'fastest of all the whales.'

We felt thrilled by our first proper sighting of whales, even from a distance. The later watch were also lucky when a pair of curious minke whales circled the ship to inspect our hull. Minkes are around half the size of fins and found in most of the world's oceans, swimming seasonally between poles and tropics. But they are still harpooned off Norway today. Years ago, I'd sailed for two weeks along the Norwegian coastline, zigzagging in and out of colossal fjords, yet we didn't see a single whale; indeed the entire lack of wildlife was surprising and disappointing. Sailing a tall ship through the Sound of Mull later that same year, I was sitting on a tiny platform at the top of the mast, taking in spectacular views of plummeting gannets and wheeling gulls, when we caught sight of a large pod of minkes, maybe twenty or so, mothers and calves too. In the bright sun, through the crystal-clear waters of the Scottish west coast, I had a God's-eye view into their lush aquatic world of kelp forests and silvery shoals of fish. I remember longing to be in the sea too, swimming alongside them. My father had once been a commercial diver, and I fancy I might have loved it too had I not watched *Jaws* at too tender an age.

Like blue whales, fins are baleen whales – toothless filter feeders. The pale ridging from the tip of their lower jaws extends down to their navels (yes, navels – of course), fluted and grooved, and vastly expandable. From their upper jaws, plates of baleen hang like a stiff moustache where their teeth might once have been in the evolutionary past, each plate dangling down more than a metre or so, and a third as wide. The whale yawns, gulping krill-laden sea into its fat throat, then presses a giant tongue to the roof of its mouth, squeezing water out through the baleen, trapping krill and fish. Baleen was the plastic of the 1800s, strong and flexible, holding umbrellas up and corsets taut. Ironically, one of the key potential threats to whales these days is the plastic that replaced baleen. Tiny particles of plastic now turn up in the Antarctic surface waters and even in sea ice and recent ice-cores. While toothed whales are more likely to beach on our shores with stomachs full of fishing gear, toothbrushes and flip-flops, baleen whales sink when dead, and any evidence of microplastics leaching toxic chemicals into their tissues, disrupting hormones, impairing development, reproduction and immune systems, remains undetected. Microplastics could be the modern silent killer of the baleens, as they filter-feed through thousands of cubic metres of seawater per day.

Heikki let out a long sigh. 'Fucking hell, this place is so beautiful.' He turned slowly, sweeping his gaze around the horizon. 'And all we do is fuck it up. All the whales we've killed, all the shit we pour into these oceans.' Heikki was a man of few words, but something about the eerie dawn had torn open the deep ecological wound that lies at the core of so many of us.

'A few hundred thousand years and you'll never know we'd been here except for a thin layer of plastic and rubble,' I said.

'Typical geologist. You can only think in millions of years. Do you believe we can still change?'

That was the big question. I hoped we could. When we damage precious ecosystems, like the Antarctic, that have taken millennia to evolve, we undermine our own chances of survival. I told Heikki that it pissed me off when people talked about *saving the planet*. The Earth had been way hotter and colder, it had survived meteor impacts and ice ages, super-volcanoes and extinctions, so it would survive us. It was our own life-support system we were destroying.

I'd learned about climate change at school in the 1970s. I went into science thinking it had all the answers, but it turned out nobody wanted answers, not if they seemed too difficult or might be too much of a bother, or if the problem just seemed all too far away. We were learning too late that it didn't work to put politicians in charge of our climate, expecting them to solve a problem that needed clever long-term thinking. They weren't the experts and often only thought as far ahead as the next election.

Heikki turned away and looked out across to the port side, his body tense. We stood quiet as the dawn glinted gold around its edges.

Janke joined us at the helm. 'What are you two looking so fed-up about?'

'Ach, the state of the planet!' I replied. 'You know, the impending apocalypse and all that.'

'Being out here focuses the mind on the big stuff, doesn't it? But look at where we are.' She circled through the compass directions. 'Live in the moment.'

'Aye, who knows?' I said, shoving my hands deep into my jacket pockets. 'We could all get swept away by a rogue wave tomorrow.'

Heikki's face cracked open with a grin. 'Well, that's fucking comforting!'

~

Your fleet heads out from South Georgia, south to that place of ice, where the glacial era still has its grip. It's your fourth whaling season, and you're working out on deck, Whaler Group VIII, the bottom of the heap. You lost your place in the quiet, clean officers' mess with its gleaming cutlery and leisurely conversation.

Last year, you arrived home full of swagger and a pocket full of money from the tips you'd earned in the officers' mess – money enough to last the summer without having to find extra work, plus some extra to put aside into your savings. But when your train pulled in to Waverley station, the grand welcome you'd expected wasn't there. Your dad stood on the platform on his own, and you knew from his look that he wasn't there with good news. Nana Lina had died.

'I thought I'd better come and tell you, son, before you got home. It happened back in January. I know how close you were.'

On the bus home, you felt the anger boil up in you. Why hadn't they let you know before? Why hadn't they sent you a telegram? You knew she was old, but you hadn't imagined there'd be a day when she wasn't there any more.

'We didn't want to upset you while you were away,' your dad said. 'It's not like you could have got back for the funeral.'

That evening, you went out to the pub, unable to sit with the rest of the family, who seemed to have moved on already. You came home horribly drunk, threw up in the front hallway and all over the bathroom. Your mum was furious.

It turned into a wretched summer. You frittered away your money in weeks, buying rounds of drinks for people in the pub – they all seemed like your best friends at the time, but when your money ran out, they disappeared. You took on labouring work, unable to find anything else, grafting day in, day out in the cement works and drinking in the pub at night.

Aunt Lottie took you aside one day. 'It's not what your nana would have wanted for you, son. Pull yourself together and stop wi' this drinking, it's just making you miserable.' But you were lost, mired in your grief and anger, not knowing what to do with it all.

By autumn, the work had dried up, and though you'd vowed never to go whaling again, you found yourself back at Salvesen's office in Bernard Street.

'Sorry, Tony,' the manager said, 'all the mess jobs are gone. If you'd have come in last week, we'd have been glad to have you. The only thing I've got left is labouring on the factory deck, but I know that's not your thing.' To his surprise, you told him you'd take it and went home to pack your bag.

Now you find yourself standing on the factory-ship deck, heading out from South Georgia, waiting for the first whales to come in. Your breath turns to mist as you coorie down into your oilskins, bought new in the slop-chest. You asked the chippy to drive some screws into the soles of your boots so you wouldn't slip on the bloody decks.

Three days out from South Georgia, and the ship is hit by an outbreak of flu; coughs and fevers run rife among the crew, and men lay confined to their bunks, those more seriously ill with pneumonia lodged in the sick-bay. But you're young, and quickly shake it off. It happens every year. The whale men isolated on South Georgia for the winter are easy targets for viruses brought in by new crews. The disease, more virulent for its incubation in the overwinterers, quickly spreads through the cramped and stuffy cabins to the rest of the men. On the way down to South Georgia, an outbreak of measles killed one of the new mess boys, fifteen and on his first trip. The ship hove to for an hour as everyone turned out for the funeral. His slender body, wrapped in a linen shroud, two harpoons folded into it on either side, slid off the rails of the ship. And then it was back to work.

The number one catcher boat, captained by gunner Arne Mikalsen, has sped ahead of the fleet towards the South Orkney Islands in the Scotia Sea, and reports back every few hours. Danny is aboard, delighted to finally be part of Arne's crew, hoping this season will bring him a good bonus. The radio signal echoes around the factory as you all listen intently for Arne's first call.

Finally, he radios in, excited and barely audible in his animation, reporting his position in code – tumbleweed, ink, donkey, Columbus – so as not to give away advantage to other fleets; there are nineteen other factory ships here, of many different nationalities. A thrill ripples through the ship. They have found a group of sperm whales. These can be taken at any time of the year as only bull sperms are found in Antarctic waters; the females live and breed further north. The fleet surges ahead, catcher boats, buoy boats and corvettes, thirsty for the first kill.

The factory men are split into two twelve-hour watches, and from now until the end of the season, the ship works twenty-four hours a day. You're on the day shift and ready yourself, blubber hook in hand, assigned to work with the flensers.

The first whale is a young male sperm – the blue and fin season hasn't begun yet. It's dragged in by a buoy boat and transferred to the aft of the factory ship. The tail flukes have been sliced off, being too wide to fit the ship's rear slipway. The big *hval kla* – a steel grab shaped to fit over the whale's tail stump – is lowered, attached by wires and controlled by five separate winchmen; the deck boss, leaning over the side of the slipway railings, uses intricate hand signals to guide them, timing the grab perfectly as the whale bounces in choppy seas. The *kla* opens like an arcade-game grabber and drops with a crash, shuddering the ship right through to the tanks in the hull. The whale is brought aboard, dragged up the slipway. As he emerges onto the plan deck, the flensers dash forward with their hockey-stick knives, angling the blades, making long slices through the thick blubber as the whale is winched past them into position. He has large circular scars across his side – sucker marks from fights with giant squid in the depths of the ocean – and the skin on his back is tyre-thick and wrinkled like a prune.

INTO THE BLUE

You and the other blubber boys set to work, dragging the white jelly-like blocks with your hooks into the steaming hatches, careful of your footing on the slippery decks lest you too fall down the hatches and into the boiling cookers below.

As you work, you remember all the things Ferguson, keen to quench your thirst for knowledge, told you about sperm whales last year. They are smart and good communicators too. Early on in the Arctic whaling boom, sperm-whale catches plummeted after the whales learned that they could escape the sail-powered ships by swimming upwind of them. The tactic, first seen in just a few whales, quickly spread through the Arctic populations, communicated to other pods via their complex language of clicks and pulses. The whales had yet to find a way to outrun the steam-powered ships though.

The flensers moan about working on sperm whales: the blubber is tough, the head nearly half the length of the body. The catcher-boat crews don't like them either. Sperm whales are aggressive and often fight back, using their big heads as battering rams, most famously sinking the whale ship *Essex* – the inspiration for *Moby-Dick*. But they are prized for their spermaceti, the wax-like oil found in a large cavity in the whale's boxy head, and worth at least twenty-five per cent more than standard blubber oil. The head is cut open at the top, and the spermaceti, nearly 400 gallons of it, is scooped out in buckets. Inside, the oil is liquid, but it solidifies on meeting the cold air. Once emptied, winch hooks are attached to the skull, and it's pulled from the carcass, splattering the remaining spermaceti over any rookie who's too close. You know this trick and stand well clear.

And then there is little left of the whale but a pile of dark meat and bones. The deck boss steps forward with a knife and notebook. He splits the belly, spilling the whale's innards onto the plan. Like cows, sperm whales have four stomachs – and over 1,000 feet of intestines, but unlike the filter-feeding baleens, they are toothed and dive for squid and cuttlefish. If he's lucky, the bosun will find ambergris too, dark waxen lumps formed around squid beaks in the whale's intestines, in the same way that grains of sand are transformed into pearls in oysters. The ambergris is sold as a fixative for perfume and worth a small fortune. You once met an old whaler scouring the Granton shore for ambergris when you were a lad; it only reaches its true worth when aged in the sea. It floats, so it can wash up on shores years after a whale has died, becoming paler with age, smelling of sandalwood and old churches, and then it is one of the most valuable natural substances on Earth.

The bosun notes the stomach contents for the biologists back home. He also pulls one of the teeth from the twenty or so on the narrow lower jaw – sperm whales don't have upper teeth, just sockets for the lower teeth to fit in to. When the teeth are sliced through, the biologists back home count the rings to tell the age of the whale. Other men take teeth too, for whittling and carving in idle hours, making scrimshaw etched with tall ships, penguins and whales. You take one and put it in your pocket. Each year you bring a few home for the family, one for each of your brothers and your sister Mary.

The lemmers and bonesawmen slice up the last of the meat and bones, and the hook boys drag it to the hatches. The butchered whale is boiled in the steam cookers below, the intestines dumped into the sea.

Soon, the blue and fin season begins, and the attentive fleet of catchers keep the factory well fed, like cats bringing in bloodied mice to drop on the kitchen floor. In return, they get fresh water, fuel and supplies. Dead whales are used as fenders, slung between the boats as they come alongside to prevent damage in the rough seas. You and the other deck boys are roped in to help the catchers load up; running errands to the slop-chest for their crews.

Once the catchers depart, the fender whales are processed too, even those that have lain alongside the ship for nearly a week, their stomachs and intestines burst into the sea. Their blubber is stripped and the rotten meat sent down into the boilers. Deep inside these fender whales, the meat is often fully cooked and charred by the heat of decomposition coupled with the insulation of the blubber. These are *burnt whales*, their middles so hot you can't even put a hand on the meat without being scalded. Even the hardiest of flensers and lemmers heave as they cut away the putrid mess. The stench on deck becomes unbearable.

The work is hard and long. Twelve-hour shifts, seven days a week, the job all-consuming – nothing but bed and work, bed and work – and soon you're exhausted, leaning in to the drudgery with little else to do and no energy to socialise, no one to talk to. You miss the officers' mess, the overheard conversations and your chats with Ferguson. You've seen him passing in the distance a few times and waved, but he didn't recognise you.

The catchers deliver the first blue whale: a female, monstrous in size compared to the sperms, as long as a train carriage and as high too. As she is dragged aboard, barely squeezing through the rear slipway, the flensers slice down her length and then, with deft flicks of their knives, cut steps into her sides so they can climb up on top, the soles of their boots, like yours, studded with screws to stop them slipping as the ship rolls beneath them. The flensers call down wire ropes dropped from the derrick above and hook them in; the blubber is peeled in long wide strips like a banana skin.

Striding among the flensers, Sinclair, the whaling inspector, dressed in a boiler suit and long rubber boots, walks the length of the whale and places a spike in the deck, lined up with the end of her tail, noting the number of notches cut into the stump (four – for number four catcher boat). He runs a measuring tape from the spike and attaches it to another placed in line with her snout. Ninety-two feet – big even for a blue – much longer than the minimum sixty feet: any less than this would be marked down as a 'short whale' and incur the wrath of the inspector, though he has little power to dish out penalties. He does, however, have the respect of the men, and a sheepish gunner would at least listen to his admonishments and promise to be more careful in future.

Once the whale is measured, Sinclair walks down her length to check her udders, giving one a firm squeeze. A gush of thick milk emerges; she is lactating and has been killed illegally. Sinclair is furious, as the calf will starve swimming alone. As he leaves to radio the number four catcher boat to have a stern word with her gunner, the whale men step forward with their mugs, squeezing out the last of this mother's milk to drink for themselves, declaring it a delicacy. The thought of it sickens you.

With the blubber stripped from the whale's top side, work stops, and the men step back for the whale to be turned. The momentary pause gives you a brief respite from the work. The flensers light half-smoked cigarettes, taking advantage of the lull. A wire rope is passed through a pulley on the deck, then over her top to attach to the fin on the other side. The winch engine fires up, and you all take cover. This is the most dangerous part, the full weight of the whale dependent on that one pulley attached to the deck. Many times it's broken loose and catapulted the width of the ship or beyond. The rope tightens, and the winch whines, straining under the weight before the whale begins to slither in her own blood. Slowly, she heaves over on to her other side, slapping back down to the deck, juddering the ship and sending scarlet rivers across the plan. The flensers jump back to work. Again, the strips of blubber are peeled, and you move in, snagging thick chunks with your large wood-handled hook, dragging them to the open hatches and into the boilers below.

Once the blubber is stripped, the flensers begin removing the baleen, slicing a hole in the centre of the whale's upper gum and passing a wire through it. As the winch lifts, the flenser cuts through the base of her gums, and when the last slice is made, he signals to the winchman, and anyone on deck runs for cover as the tons of baleen are torn from the roof of her mouth, swung out across the deck and dumped overboard. Now that plastic has replaced it, baleen is no longer valuable enough to warrant its passage home. The jawbone is next, winched forward for the bonesawmen. And then the tongue – huge and slippery, the weight of three good-sized horses, spread wide across the deck. It is quickly sliced and dragged away into the cookers too.

The head flenser nods to the winchman, and her remains are dragged to the forward plan where lemmers – also with hockey-stick knives – strip her flesh. Her ribs are sliced off and winched away, each twice as tall as a man, and then the steam-driven bonesaw slices up her spine. Her liver is removed to its own special boiler, the oil full of vitamin D, vital for preventing rickets in children back home. Again, the deck boss comes with his knife and notebook to split the stomach, spilling her last meal – a thick school of half digested krill – across the deck. He cuts out her ovaries, the size of footballs, to pickle in barrels for a London biologist who pays threepence a pair. Over the course of the season it adds up to a good bonus. The last of her meat and bones are fed to the boilers, and her stomach and intestines are cast overboard, feeding the squabbling flocks of speckled cape pigeons and killer whales. The plan deck is hosed down. And then there is nothing left of this giant mother, only yesterday alive and swimming with her calf, now stripped down by men to turn into fertiliser, animal feed and tanks of oil.

~

'Ten point four knots!' said Heikki, and we cheered, hitting our record of the day. Each watch competed to get us into double-digit speeds. It felt like we were flying. Ocean-fresh cloudless skies and strong easterly winds smoothed our passage towards South Orkney.

We passed sixty degrees south and into the Antarctic Treaty zone. Here, all land and ice are protected by international agreement. Prior to the 1959 treaty, everyone wanted a piece of this continent, with claims and counter-claims for sovereignty, but in a remarkable show of cooperation, the disputing nations came together to protect Antarctica from territorial squabbles and military action, dedicating it to the pursuit of scientific research and collaboration. However tenuous it might seem at times, the Antarctic Treaty is a unique example of how countries *can* work together to protect our most fragile ecosystems.

Just after midday, a loud squawking from the starboard side fetched my thoughts from the horizon. A chinstrap penguin swam in circles around the ship, thinking us a passing iceberg, keen to climb aboard for a rest. Chinstraps are black-capped and backed, but white around the eyes and along the tops of their dark beaks. A thin black line runs right around the underside of their chin like the tie of a bonnet. The islands of the Scotia Sea are prime breeding ground for chinstraps. We shifted rail to rail, port to starboard, watching the penguin scramble like a baby bird fallen from its nest. He stayed with us for most of the day, becoming increasingly annoyed and insistent as the wind strengthened and our speed increased. By late afternoon another joined him. After a few more attempts to jump aboard and a loud disagreement, they abandoned us for a passing growler and a much easier landing spot, where they stood preening away their indignity.

We reached Signy Island, a tiny scrap of rubbled rock and ice, four miles long and three miles wide. Part of the South Orkney archipelago, it lies just inside the Antarctic Treaty zone and has been home to a British research station since 1947, though now it is manned in summer only by a crew of five. Nearby Laurie Island houses the Argentinian Orcadas Base. The South Orkney Islands have a muddled history, first discovered by sealers, American-born Nathaniel Palmer and British-born George Powell, in 1821. Two years later, an expedition led by British sailor and sealer James Weddell visited the islands to re-map them and discovered Signy, though it wasn't named until Norwegian whaler and inventor of the factory ship rear slipway, Petter Sørlle, surveyed the island in 1912 and 1913 and christened it after his wife. Laurie Island was mapped by William Speirs Bruce on the Scottish National Antarctic Expedition, and he set up a weather station and base there in 1903, but the British Government refused to fund its continuation. Bruce offered it to the Argentines on the condition that they ran it as a scientific base. The Argentines agreed and set up Orcadas. It has been permanently manned since.

In 1908, with the Klondike of industrial whaling ramping up in the Antarctic, Britain rued its decision to forgo funding for the Laurie Island base and issued a formal claim over the entire South Orkney archipelago, including Laurie Island. The Argentines did not challenge it at the time, a move interpreted by the British as acceptance of their sovereignty, but the Argentines later strengthened their own claim by setting up a wireless telegraph station and post office without British permission. The two countries have been bickering ever since, although, with the signing of the Antarctic Treaty, they have officially put their differences aside, though both still maintain a foot in the door – research stations and post offices being the current weapons of choice.

The islands breached into view, tiny in the distance against the vast sea and sky. The horizon slipped away at the edges like the curve of an albatross's wings. At first we only saw a distant glow at the cloud-base, a sign of ice – clouds above the sea are darker – then mountain peaks, sharp as puppy teeth, appeared, flanked by stranded icebergs just as tall.

Though a landing was doubtful, dependent on good weather and pack ice, we busied ourselves vacuuming pockets and rucksacks and cleaning our boots so we didn't transfer seeds from South Georgia, where invasive dandelions in particular had already taken hold. When we finally edged into Factory Cove – the site of yet another old whaling station – conditions for landing appeared more favourable.

The five British Antarctic Survey staff stood dockside, waving as our crew ferried us ashore. 'You're our only visitors this year,' they beamed as we stepped onto their small wooden pier. Alex Taylor, tall, rugged, huge-handed and wearing a full beard and beanie hat, worked as the guide and logistics technician for the BAS team. He looked like he wouldn't think twice about striding out in a blizzard to rescue you from the wrong side of the island should you find yourself in difficulties while counting penguins one afternoon. He took us on a tour of the research station, but there wasn't a whole lot to see: green, corrugated, steel frame sheds storing generators, equipment and samples, and the long, low shoreside building where the accommodation and offices stood.

'Come in, come in.' Alex waved us inside the end of a building kitted out like a small city office – whiteboards, in-trays, out-trays and PCs. At the other end lay small dormitories, not included in the tour. They'd pushed furniture aside and covered the floor in plastic sheeting to protect the carpet tiles from our wet boots. Two desks shoved together formed a long table spread with colourful T-shirts, mugs, badges and postcards – a makeshift gift shop of Signy Island memorabilia. In an adjacent room, field assistant Stacey Adlard, the latest in a long line of research scientists counting penguins on Signy, doubled as postmaster, issuing the island's own stamps for our postcards, again complete with the queen's head. Lex sat alongside her, stamping our passports, proof of our visit to this snippet of the empire.

The challenges of climate and accessibility made the research work on Signy especially difficult. The staff undergo intensive survival and health and safety training before they arrive. All supplies have to be shipped in – there is nowhere to land a plane – so they need to be self-sufficient for the full five or six months that the station operates. If anything breaks – plumbing, electrical, structural, mechanical – they have to have the means to fix it. Half the island is covered in ice, and gales can whip up in a heartbeat, so getting around the island is an expedition in itself. Signy is among the world's most difficult and expensive locations to study science, and yet it is critical for understanding our changing planet.

Gentoo, Adélie and chinstrap penguins all breed on Signy. The gentoos have done well, but the Adélies and chinstraps not so much. Untangling the ups and downs of populations is complex in any ecosystem, but the logistics mean it is especially difficult here. Gentoo penguins are opportunistic feeders, living on a mixed diet of krill, fish and squid, whereas Adélies and chinstraps live mainly on krill. After the decimation of the whales, Adélies and chinstraps both did well, with populations growing rapidly in the face of surplus krill, but in the 1970s the trend reversed, and numbers of both declined steeply in the region. Rapid warming diminished the sea ice, long thought to make conditions more favourable for chinstraps, but it's not that simple. Krill numbers in the region declined too, by as much as eighty per cent; they depend on sea ice to breed. To complicate matters, there was a huge influx of fur seals, young males in particular spilling over from the breeding grounds of South Georgia. They now gather in huge colonies on South Orkney's shores, increasing competition for a dwindling food source.

Polar ecosystems are typically stressed and fragile; the climate is extreme and prone to wild fluctuations from natural change and ecological accidents. Huge chunks of ice-shelf can drift into islands like these, cutting nesting penguins from their food source, altering local climate and changing sea-water salinity. Populations might collapse in a matter of a season or two but may also be quick to recover. In the long term, these ecosystems are relatively stable, having survived tens of thousands, if not millions of years. The more insidious threat of human-induced climate change is a bigger challenge, with complex tipping points and feedback loops. Untangling short-term natural fluctuations from the less reversible impacts of humans is vitally important, and good science from the dedicated staff at BAS is critical.

While we toured the research station, the other three BAS staff took up Klaas's offer to tour *Europa*. Our crew, experts in showing off the ship, first circled the Zodiacs around the bay to silhouette her against the BAS staff's ice-strewn summer home. Meanwhile, we wandered freely but under strict instruction not to cross the moss banks, thought to be thousands of years old but already deteriorating under the influx of fur seals.

I made my way to the end of the peninsula, passing another makeshift graveyard with five upstanding white wooden crosses. This time I could not go in. How many more young men had these islands swallowed and not returned home?

Kate stood on a rock near the shore like an Antony Gormley statue, staring out to sea.

I sidled up beside her. She looked sad. 'You okay?'

She turned towards me, her mind still at sea. 'My husband would have loved it here. I really miss him at times like this. Grief is so pervasive.'

Nearby, a pair of Adélie penguins primped each other's slick coats, their flat-topped black heads punctuated by an icy ring around their eyes. Most of these penguins mate for life, working in close partnership to rear their chicks on stony nests.

We stood in silence for a while. Tiny waves lapped at our feet, and we gazed across the bay dotted equally with islands and icebergs. 'God, I'd love to do something like this,' said Kate. 'Spend the summer in the middle of the Southern Ocean, counting penguins. No shops, no cars, just looking out at this view. I bet it's different every day. Icebergs coming and going, the changing weather, the colour of the sea. Just to be peaceful while the land and sea swirl around you.'

I wondered if this really was a place to find peace, or whether, like South Georgia, it was already too full of loss.

~

The pace is relentless. A constant stream of whales is delivered to the factory slipway. You work quickly and efficiently to keep up. On 23 December, fifty-two whales are caught – six blues, four humpbacks, three sperms and thirty-nine fins. There is barely time to catch your breath.

The whole Antarctic fleet consists of three British factory ships, ten Norwegian, three Japanese, one Russian, one South African, one Dutch and one registered in Panama, owned by Aristotle Onassis, plus all the catcher boats, buoy boats and supply vessels. The total season quota is 16,000 blue whale units, though not all whales are created equal in the eyes of the Whaling Commission: two fins, two and a half humpbacks, or six sei whales equal one blue. But the quota only applies to those voluntarily signed up to the international agreements. The Onassis ship, the *Olympic Challenger*, can take as many whales as it wants, including calves and pregnant females.

On the deck of the *Southern Venturer*, a blackboard tallies the number of whales brought in by each catcher boat. Whales still to be processed are towed from the slipway. You're woken in your bunk one morning by a cabin-mate on the night watch. He tells you about the whale they've found alive, dragged astern by the stump of its tail. You go up on deck to find a gaggle of men standing around the slipway. It's a young male blue. He's barely moving but definitely alive, his pectoral fins flailing. He is puffing and blowing through giant flared nostrils, but shallow breaths, not the usual great spout of a blue. When the night crew noticed, they'd radioed a catcher boat to come in and harpoon him – to put him out of his misery – and the men are waiting for it to arrive. The ship's bell rings for the start of your shift, and you begin work on the other whales. Half an hour later, the catcher comes in, and the loud bang of a close-firing harpoon makes you start. The dull explosion of a grenade follows.

The factory is having a bumper harvest, the decks busy night and day. In the brief Antarctic nights the men work under bright arc lights, steam coming off both whales and men. The sea teems with whales, and the Norwegian gunners are doing a superb job of killing them. Each evening, as you sit down for your meal, all you hear is talk of production, the number of barrels processed – 15,000 so far – and though the oil is no longer stored in barrels, it's still the standard unit of measurement. The factory ships are given targets by Salvesen each season, calculated as the average production over the last three years. Half the crew's wages depend on it, but it's a con. If the target is met, though you'll return home well paid, next year's will increase, making it harder to reach. This year's target is 159,000 barrels.

Beneath the hatches pockmarking the plan deck lie the blubber and meat pots, ten feet in diameter and twenty deep. They're tended to by around eighty men who coax and nurture their boilers, check steam pressures and ensure everything runs smoothly. With so much at stake, efficiency is vital if they are to squeeze out every last drop of oil. In heavy seas, it's a tough job to dodge the scalding steam and keep the machines running, but when it's calm the men relax a little, read books, and keep an occasional eye on the dials. The men down here are voracious readers, some getting through a book each day: natural history, thrillers, politics, languages and Shakespeare. There are few subjects on which they are not knowledgeable. Any time on their hands is well spent.

On the lower deck, beneath the boilers, liquid is drained from the cookers and centrifuged to separate out the oil. Samples are taken for checking and grading by the two on-board chemists in their specially fitted lab high on the poop deck. The oils are analysed for vitamin content, viscosity and purity, but the chemists are also tasked with inventing more creative uses for the whales. New mineral oils and synthetic fertilisers are emerging, and whaling, once serving a market in need of products, is fast producing products in need of a market.

Once graded, the oil is poured into a freshly cleaned tank on the bottom deck. The cavernous tanks hold both fuel oil and whale oil. Successful operations rely on quick cleaning of tanks once depleted of fuel oil so they can be refilled with the processed whale oil. The tank gangs spray high-pressure hoses of scalding water to remove the fuel, but some of it lurks under the girders and heating coils, so the men have to scrub and scrape with paraffin until the chemists are satisfied with the job. The tank gangs are paid a good bonus, but you don't volunteer. There are too many accidents in the tanks.

On Christmas Eve, you feel the rush of excitement when the catchers come in to load up on supplies, their crews wheedling as much alcohol as they can from the factory storeman. The mess rooms and saloons are decorated with tinsel and cotton-snow, though only the upper echelons get time off to celebrate. The rest of you use your saved-up rum ration for a wee celebration in one of the cabins after your shift, but that's about it.

You remember Christmas last year in the officers' mess. The galley ran full pelt cooking two types of traditional Christmas fare: turkey for the Brits, *lapskaus* for the Norwegians. At dinner, the officers were all upstanding as the king was toasted, and then again for the other king, and no one asked whether King George or King Haakon was toasted first. The men all wore paper crowns and got drunk on fine whisky. Your meagre celebration in the dingy cabin is all too depressing in comparison.

There's an hour's holiday for you and the other Scots on New Year's Eve. You down your weekly tot of Navy Rum, but it's not much, and not enough for many. Most of the crew smuggled on extra supplies at Tenerife, but it hasn't lasted and the ship is drying out. Tempers are short and workdays long. There's been no news from home all season, no letters, and you are beginning to feel isolated, your conversation dwindling.

By mid January, the weather improves, the greyness lifts, and the sea and icebergs glitter under a bright sun. Catchers dart to and fro, bringing in whale after whale; when the weather is good, the fishing is good. Four hundred blue whale units processed, and ten weeks to go. A chalkboard on the plan deck keeps score for the catcher boats, each whale tallied to the boat that caught it. You hope the Antarctic quota will be caught early this year so you can head home sooner.

One evening, the galley crew serves up strawberries, brought from home and frozen in the stores. They taste as fresh as the ones from your family berry-picking outings back home. You feel the leaden weight of homesickness creeping in, thinking back to the strain and awkwardness of your departure. Your mum and Aunt Lottie at the end of their tether with you. Your dad stern, telling you he hoped a season of graft would sort you out and to come back in better spirits. You wince at the thought of your behaviour towards them, regretting the drinking and vowing to do better this year when you get home. You sell your rum ration for a beautifully carved and mounted whale's tooth as a present for your mum.

Passing the South Sandwich Islands, you're treated to a spectacular show. Thule, an active volcano, splutters smoke and bright lava into the air. Work pauses briefly, and you all crowd the decks to watch and feel the booming explosions deep in your chest. The stories you'll have to tell when you get home – you can just imagine the wide-eyed looks of your younger brothers.

Working seven days a week, with no weekends to look forward to, is proving hard. The shifts are exhausting. Nerves are frayed. Arguments, and sometimes fights, break out, mainly among the younger lads still trying to establish their place in the pecking order. Robertson the doctor is kept busy with queues of men outside his door for morning and evening surgeries. The flensers and lemmers regularly suffer infected cuts; even the slightest scratch can turn septic among the bloody conditions of the plan deck. The engineers, refusing to wear safety glasses, get metal splinters in their eyes, and the men on the factory floor are often scalded by steam cookers. But there are more serious accidents too. The first mate on one of the catchers has his legs mangled below the knees. A harpooned fin whale swam beneath the boat, catching the line around the spinning propeller, slicing it through so it ricocheted the remaining rope back onto the deck and around the man's legs. Robertson boards the catcher to treat him.

The man has been laid out in a cramped cabin deep in the bowels of the boat, well dosed on rum for the pain. His wounds are critical, and he is transferred to the sick bay on the factory ship. The doctor informs the Salvesen office that the man should be transferred to Montevideo and flown home for proper treatment as a matter of urgency, but they decline, and he is taken back on a catcher to Leith Harbour to lie in his plasters until the end of the season before enduring the month-long voyage home on the factory ship.

To cheer you up, the film *Green for Danger* is shown one evening – only the second film you've had since the season began. The black-and-white movie flickers in the dark mess room. Men gather, sitting on chairs, on the floor. You perch on a table at the back, watching young nurses fall in love with handsome doctors as an orchestra plays dramatic music. The actors stare meaningfully into the distance as Alastair Sim plays a laid-back detective trying to solve two tepid murders.

The supply of blue and fin whales dwindles, and it's mostly smaller sei whales caught now. They yield much less oil than the blues, so production slows. The weather is cold and sleet-ridden, the scenery nothing but whale intestines.

At 4 a.m. one morning, the ship's alarm bells ring, persistent and loud. You're woken and assemble on the icy deck to find out that the head chemist was seen jumping overboard, and though the factory is turned around, he is not found. A chill runs through the ship. Morale falls to an all-time low. To make matters worse, the *Southern Garden*, due in with the mail, doesn't show, so there are still no letters or news from home. Your disappointment turns to dejection.

~

The morning after our visit to Signy, progress slowed to a crawl. Slushy growlers hung on or just below the sea surface. Relieved of our helm duties, we put extra lookouts on the bow as Klaas and Janke navigated the way through. The tension felt palpable, the smell all pervading as the ice trickle-dripped around us. We passed larger bergs, clear rivulets of meltwater running from their skirts. Black bands of rubble released ancient grit to the ocean floor.

In the Antarctic, most icebergs are snapped from flat shelves spilling out over the edges of the continent. They are often compared in size to small countries (Belgium or Luxembourg), English counties (Sussex or Kent), or some division of Wales. These whopping ice counties are named when they first split. As if a crosshair were sighted at the South Pole on a map of Antarctica, the continent is divided into four quadrants, with the top left over the Weddell Sea and the Antarctic Peninsula (between longitude 0 degrees and 90 degrees west). This is where icebergs prefixed with an A are born. Moving anticlockwise through the quadrants, the Bs are from the Amundsen and Eastern Ross Sea (longitude 90 west to 180 degrees); Cs are from the Western Ross Sea and Wilkes Land (longitude 180 to 90 degrees east); and Ds from the Amery Ice Shelf and Eastern Weddell Sea (longitude 90 degrees east to 0 degrees). Then the bergs are numbered sequentially. As they break apart, the names are further subdivided by suffixing letters in alphabetical order for each part larger than ten nautical miles. Smaller than this, they drift in anonymity.

Iceberg A68 calved from the Larsen C ice-shelf in July 2017 under the dark cover of the polar winter night, but satellite radars witnessed its split, and, soon after, a small block broke off. The remaining berg was named A68A. Over the next two and a half years, satellites tracked A68A as it spun northwards out of the Weddell Sea gyre – the clockwise rotation of currents, pack ice and bergs that scour into the eastern belly of the Antarctic Peninsula – towards South Georgia, an island it uncannily resembled in size and shape. Scientists watched, anxious that it might ground on the island's shallow shelves, altering local currents, water temperature and salinity. As the berg neared South Georgia, it veered southeast at the last moment, following local currents before breaking apart, its fragments waltzing off and named all the way up to M.

Bits of ice-shelf were easy to spot: flat-topped, long and blocky, layered thin with compressed snow like fine-grained sandstone, weathered like rocky islands, forming cliffs up to 100 metres high, wave-cut platforms, coves and caves, arches and stacks – the carving of a coastline fast-forwarded. Eroded by the sea, their centres of gravity shifted, they tilted and lurched drunken in the waves; some even overturned, their undersides smooth as granite sculpted into sleek Henry Moore curves.

As we nudged our way further south, the work grew tougher and the air colder. Icicles dripped from the rigging. Hemp ropes froze, locked in glistening shells of ice. I sat in the deckhouse, wet clothing strung from every heater and hook, reading about James Cook's search for the Antarctic continent in 1772. He'd picked the worst possible time to go – the Earth had wobbled into a mini-ice age, and increased volcanic dust in the atmosphere had cooled temperatures further. As Cook sailed south, he'd been turned back by pack ice repeatedly. At fifty-four degrees south, the ship's ropes froze to the size of men's arms, they struggled to brace the yards or hoist sails – and of course, they had no engines for back-up.

Even when the whalers sailed here, it would have been brutal to work in such conditions, clothed only in wet wool and oilskins in the days before fleece or Gore-Tex. I was beginning to find sympathy as I imagined their voyages on these brutal seas in those tiny catcher boats like the *Petrel* thrust up on Grytviken's shore.

That night, asleep in my bunk, I felt the ship slow to a stop. I had grown used to ignoring changes in the ship's angle and speed as I slept, but this sudden halt startled me awake. Minutes later, Kate burst in. 'We've hit pack ice.'

5

Antarctic Blue

Kate could be a little dramatic, so I wasn't fazed by her sense of alarm, but as I was due on watch at midnight, I hauled on my waterproofs, climbed out onto the icy deck and watched my breath furl up to the rigging. The half-light tinted my vision a ghostly blue. The cold pressed into my face. On all sides, ice smothered the sea, pancaked, rucked and rafted, hugging the rise and fall of a sluggardly swell. And the smell of it! All-pervading, sharp and stale. It reminded me of those days at home when, with a sigh, I'd have to defrost the freezer and use trays of boiling water to melt the thick shelves of ice – it was *that* smell, sweet and sour, cold to the top of the sinuses.

Our world lay poised between two states: liquid and solid – water and ice. The molecules could go either way: lose all notion of solidity and mingle anonymous back to the ocean, or, with a breath of icy wind, become crystal-locked and hard-frosted into order and stability.

We skirted the outer edges of the Weddell Sea, a few degrees north of the place the *Endurance* sank after being caught in the giant ice-gyre. This sea is well known for its abrupt temperature gradients and the extraordinary clarity of the air: it compresses distances, creates shifting visions and liquid boundaries. Mirages are common, land appears where it is not, and the sun might set multiple times in a day. Within hours, loose ice might harden and pack solid with no warning. Shackleton's ship was not the first to be trapped and sunk in these shape-shifting waters, nor the last.

Our ship bumped and shivered along at her slowest speed. Deep groans reverberated along her sides, grumbling the story of how growlers had earned their name, but some squealed and squeaked too, and smaller lumps knocked their way down the length of our hull like a builder might tap at a wall for weakness, though he would find none in our sturdy steel ship.

I stood at the rails, hypnotised by the vivid turquoise lapping the wide platforms around each growler. Nothing else in nature holds this colour, except perhaps the feathers of bright tropical birds, though not with this depth, this translucency. The waters of the Weddell Sea possess astonishing clarity; objects as deep as eighty metres can be seen from the rails of a ship on a bright day. Its huge circular gyre keeps the cold clear waters protected from warmer currents seeping in from the north. Sea ice formation, though waxing and waning through the year, concentrates salinity in the surrounding water, making it dense, drawing cold down to the ocean floor, blocking warmer currents rising beneath the ice-sheets fringing the Weddell Sea's shores. Year-round pack ice supports a vital food source for juvenile krill too: ice algae. Each winter, the extent of sea ice determines krill numbers for the following summer: the more ice, the more krill. Prions, cape and Antarctic petrels swarm its edges. Whales feed like sharks around coral reefs.

But this sea is changing. The warming climate over the past few decades has caused the westerly winds around

Antarctica to strengthen and the circumpolar currents to shift south, encroaching into the Weddell Sea. The gyre has shrunk but intensified its spin, drawing in warmer waters from the north. Stormier weather, higher winds and waves are breaking up the diminishing ice, already a fifth smaller in surface area than the extents recorded by whalers in the 1950s. As it wanes, turning the sea from white to blue, less sunlight is reflected, warming the water further, creating a positive feedback loop. But the bottom of the Weddell Sea hides a more insidious threat. Since the Industrial Revolution, the global oceans have absorbed more than ninety per cent of the heat trapped in the atmosphere by greenhouse gases, and the depths of the Weddell Sea are warming five times faster than anywhere else on the planet. With less sea ice on the surface, there is less of the cold dense saline water raining down from above to block these encroaching currents. Ice-shelves fringing this coastline act as buttresses to the glaciers and ice-sheets draining this side of the Antarctic continent, and they are beginning to thin. Once they fail, a vital tipping point is crossed, and runaway, irreversible and unstoppable melting is likely to begin. The global temperature rise needed to reach this tipping point is minuscule. It's likely to be the difference between limiting warming by the end of the century to less than two degrees Celsius above pre-industrial levels. On our current emissions trajectory, according to the Global Action Tracker in 2022, warming could reach up to 2.6 degrees Celsius even if current policy pledges and promises are kept, and much higher if they are not. Climate science is not exact, though: there are too many unknowns. Tipping points and feedback loops are difficult to account for in the models, but the predictions are dire. The Antarctic is the big wild card, with the potential to raise global sea-levels by between four and seven metres, and though changes of those magnitudes are some way off, what we do *now* will determine the trajectory of sea-level changes for millennia to come.

Jordi, the Spanish deckhand and marine guide, perched on the foremast yard, his face pinched with cold and concentration. As we leaned quiet and straight-armed on the rails, his instructions broke the silence, echoing around the ship from his handheld radio.

'Left after the cauliflower one. Now right, past the one with the penguins on top.'

We nudged forward into the night and, after a tense few hours, emerged into open water once more, abandoned our southerly course and headed west, towards Elephant Island. We hauled our sails into the mist, though barely a breath of wind troubled them. I took over the helm. The thrum of the engine vibrated through my feet and into my chest. We were going nowhere slowly, which perfectly suited this eerie indigo morning.

At 4 a.m., as we handed over to the next watch, a loud sound on the starboard side startled me. Uncannily close, it was like the pneumatic brakes of a lorry. Then more, from port and stern. Misty cones ruptured the still air: whale breath.

A large pod of fin whales surrounded our ship, their razor-like spines slicing up through the sea as they burst their breath to the dawn. They drifted around us, indifferent and trusting. I rushed to the rails to watch one rise off our stern. A silvered head preceded its gaping nostrils, and a fishy smir gusted into the air around me before the whale dived sleek beneath our ship.

Soon they overtook us, leaving my gravity-sagged face peering down into the whale's domain as I watched white trails spiral from our rudder. I envied them their three-dimensional freedom, flying through viscous seas. I'd always loved being in water, loosed from the heft of my body, tumbling and turning, looking up through the watery blue into bright daylight or sinking down into the quiet depths. 'Bury me at sea,' I'd always told my family, wistfully.

'We'll chuck you off the side of a CalMac ferry if you're lucky,' they'd reply.

We'd seen more fin whales than any others on our trip. Named for their prominent spines, they are closely related to blue whales – a little smaller, but with the same sleek outline. Hybrids of the two are not unheard of. As annual visitors to these Antarctic waters, fin whales gorge on krill through the long summer days, fattening up before returning to lower latitude breeding grounds during the southern winters. They never meet their cousins, the northern fins, whose migrations follow the boreal seasons instead.

In Antarctic waters alone, around 700,000 fin whales are estimated to have been killed in the twentieth century. Prior to this, they were rarely hunted, being too fast; only steam power and exploding harpoons made them viable prey. Perhaps as few as 15,000 to 38,000 survive today, and even if no other factors impact their recovery, they will still only be at half their pre-whaling numbers by the end of the twenty-first century.

Fin whales are sensitive creatures. It's long been known that the age of a whale at death could be counted in the layers of wax accumulated in their ear canals. Like tree rings, the layers grow with the seasons, lean dark ones alternating with pale summer-fed fat ones. Sitting in archives and museum basements around the world are drawers full of these earwax plugs, each the girth and length of a church candle, collected by biologists on whaling ships and, more recently, from strandings. Scientists from Baylor University in Texas had the clever idea of analysing this earwax. They gathered plugs from fin, blue and humpback whales and went about the tedious task of scraping minute samples from over 1,000 accumulated layers of earwax using ceramic scalpels under a microscope. Each layer was analysed for cortisol, a common stress hormone in mammals. In the same way that climate records are proxied from ice cores, the team built a detailed, 146-year record of whale stress. Viewed alongside the data for historical whaling catches, the graphs matched almost perfectly; it was clear that the more whaling in any given year, the higher the whales' cortisol levels. Fin whales had the highest cortisol levels of all. Whale stress peaked in the 1960s, when whaling was at an all-time high, but after the Marine Mammal Protection Act came into force in 1972 and put an end to most whaling, stress levels plummeted. Whale calm was restored.

More recently, whale stress levels have begun to climb again, now as a result of higher sea temperatures and shipping noise. We still know little about where fin whales breed; there is no single place they congregate. Instead, they rely on the low, pulsing songs of males to attract a mate. Shipping noise means their songs are drowned out and can no longer be heard over long distances. In the Texas study, they also measured environmental toxins in the earwax. These chemical biographies showed increasing traces of pesticides and flame retardants, especially in the first six months of the whales' lives before weaning from their mother's milk, where these toxins are most concentrated.

Our ship chugged through into the dawn as we left behind the pack ice of the Weddell Sea, heading for Elephant Island.

The whales had felt so otherworldly, so othertimely. The memory of their hulk lingered for the rest of the day.

~

It's late January, cold, overcast and sleety, the kind of day you hate the most. One of the young mess boys comes to find you as you haul great chunks of blubber to the hatches. The boy picks his way around pools of blood congealing on the deck. The factory has been on a full cook for eight days straight, the work non-stop. Your back hurts, your shoulders hurt, your hands are raw and cold, and your clothes wet through.

'The chief steward wants to see you,' the mess boy says.

At the end of your shift, you clean up and make your way up to the officers' mess, hoping a position has come up and you can go back to your old job. The smell of cigars and whisky feels warm and familiar as you enter. The hushed clink of cutlery being laid out contrasts to the grating noise of bone-saws on deck.

'Tony,' he greets you. 'Good to see you. God, you look exhausted. How are you doing?'

You exchange pleasantries with him, ask after his family.

'The *Southern Soldier* needs a deck and galley boy,' he says. 'Their boy is sick. I know you've an iron stomach and work hard, plus you've got your deck experience this year. It'll give you a bit of a change, and they've a good gunner on board so you should be in for a nice bonus. You want to go?'

You know he feels sorry for you and would have you back in the officers' mess in a heartbeat, but this might be the next best thing. A chance on a catcher. You agree.

'Good man.' He pats you on the back. 'She's coming in this evening. Get your bag packed and be ready.'

As you leave the mess, Ferguson walks in. He does a double-take, not fully recognising you at first. 'Tony, lad! I didn't know you were here this season. Where have you been hiding?'

You tell him how you missed out on your usual job and have been working on deck, but you're transferring to the *Southern Soldier*.

'Working the plan's a shitty job, Tony. Never mind, you'll enjoy life on the *Soldier*. Much more exciting than working on the factory. They've a bloody good gunner this year. They're in second place.'

He shakes your hand and wishes you good luck, but as you walk away, he calls after you.

'Tony, hang on! I've a book for you. Let's walk up to my cabin now and get it. Give you something to read if the fishing's bad.' You follow Ferguson, and he gives you a detailed run-down of the season's production figures. It doesn't mean much to you, but you nod politely. You know this is his favourite topic. At his cabin, he hands you the book: *The White Continent* by Thomas R. Henry is embossed in bold letters on its pale blue cover. At the bottom, a photo shows a giant glacier slaking out between mountain peaks.

'You'll like it, I think.' He grips your hand in the firm double handshake he gave you the first time you met him outside the doctor's office in Bernard Street. 'Take good care of yourself on the *Soldier*, Tony. Hellish fun, but dangerous bloody boats.'

Your excitement is tinged with apprehension. The catchers are tiny for the size of the seas they sail on. Rust runs the length of their grey hulls, and they lean hard into each turn. They are small, unstable boats that any rogue wave might capsize – and sometimes do. If, in the thrill of the chase, a boat is steered too hard and hit on the beam by the swell, it stands little chance. You remember a few seasons ago the sinking of the catcher boat *Simbra* – you knew some of the men that died, had served them in the mess on your first season. John Leask from Shetland had been a deck boy on the *Simbra* at the time. He told you the story as you worked together in the galley one night on the voyage down to South Georgia last year.

'We'd come alongside the *Venturer* to stock up on oil supplies, but she was offloading to a tanker at the time, so they sent us away until the following day,' he said. 'We weren't too steady without fuel in the bunkers, but we carried on fishing anyway. We'd caught and flagged a couple of whales when I took my turn in the lookout barrel. I bloody hated that job, freezing cold.'

John sighted a pod of fins, and the *Simbra* gave chase, but the whales disappeared into pack ice. The skipper ordered a turn about to pick up the whales already caught. The mate turned the catcher to starboard, into the wind, but she leaned hard over, and, without ballast, she just kept going. 'I had to come down the rigging head-first on my hands and knees,' John said. The catcher was right on her side, water pouring in through the hatches.

The men had to jump into the freezing seas as the *Simbra* went under. Seven men, including John, made it into the lifeboat, but it was full of water from the rough seas. They were soaked. 'I could hear the other deck boy, a young lad from Edinburgh, he was, shouting my name over and over, calling for help, but we couldn't reach him.'

Three of the men in the lifeboat quickly died of exposure and were put over the side. The catcher had gone down so fast they'd been unable to send out a distress call. After an hour, a ship missed their flares, leaving the men stranded in the life boat up to their knees in water. The other three men died within hours, leaving only John to sit out the night.

'I must have dozed off. I was woken up by the sound of a harpoon firing. It was another catcher, one of ours. I used a bucket on top of an oar to get their attention.'

John was rescued – the only survivor.

That evening, the *Southern Soldier* comes alongside the factory, and a line is strung from the winch boom over to the catcher. Hanging from the line, a wicker basket transfers supplies and men. The catcher bounces in the sea alongside the more stable factory ship, so a dead whale is slung between them to soften any collision. You're glad to see the other boy winched across to the factory first. The basket is guided in, landing square on the deck. Your heart races. You've never done this before. You throw in your kit bag and climb into the basket, crouching down, and reach up to hold onto the sides with both hands. The deck boss gives the signal, and the basket jerks high into the air then out over the wide gap between the boats, over the dead whale, then on to the catcher deck. Experienced hands guide it in, and you land with a thud. You're heaved out by two men and set down on the deck. The gunner at the helm, dressed in grubby yellow oilskins and a fur-lined leather hat, gives the signal for the men to cast off; he is anxious to get fishing again. The hawsers are released, and with a thick belch of black smoke from her single aft funnel, the *Soldier* wheels to port and races back to her hunting grounds.

You feel the steep rise and fall of the boat beneath you – so different from the rock-steady deck of the *Venturer*. The speed is thrilling, her bow lifted by the power of her stern engine, a churn of white water in her wake.

The other deck galley boy on board, Eck – short for Alex – from Edinburgh, shows you to your shared cabin. Though the work on the catchers is the best paid, they also have the worst living conditions. In anything but flat seas, waves wash over the decks, so hatches are battened down and scuttles closed, making the cramped spaces below fetid and stuffy. Wet clothing sways from every available hook or is piled in heaps on the floor. You dump your bag and make your way up to the small galley, where Eck gives you a run-down of your duties on board. You've to prepare meals, make coffee, clean the men's cabins and toilets and be out on deck to help when needed. Shifts are four hours on and four off, around the clock. Men sleep in catnaps, rarely getting a proper rest. 'And if you hear the harpoon, you'd best be out quick,' Eck says.

The next morning, you're sent up to the barrel on look-out. You climb the shrouds strung from the outer edge of the boat to the top of the mast. Fixed between them, ratlines form a ladder of sorts – a wobbly, moving, swaying ladder. You're terrified but don't want to lose face. When you make it into the barrel, your heart pounds in your ears, your mouth dry.

The mast sways side to side, the horizon lurches around you, but soon you settle in, rubbing your hands against the cold, hunkering down out of the wind, just sticking out your head to scan the seas for whale spouts. The view is spectacular. The huge barrier icebergs tower above the catcher on a scale the envy of any cathedral. At a distance, they appear white, but up close they're suffused with hues of blues and greens. You've never seen such vivid colours. Thunderous cracks resound as larger bergs split their steep faces, crashing great chunks of ice into the sea. They bounce back in huge towers before settling into the brash-strewn waters. On the factory ship, you barely had the chance to look out over the rails, and the ship didn't venture deep into the ice. But on the catcher, the seascape is immediate and piercing. This is the Antarctica you'd hoped to see when you read those adventure stories as a boy.

You look down at the gunner on the helm. He gives you a wide smile before returning to scan the seas for whales.

~

As we closed in, Elephant Island breached the horizon, thick ice dripping down its sides. It had not been on our itinerary, but the pack ice had pushed us further west than expected, and to please the Shackleton fans, the crew had added it to our schedule. I'd read so much about Shackleton's men on Elephant Island but never thought I'd see it.

The soft seas and serrated islands confounded my senses. Chunks of ice nodded in hues of sky, and slush bobbed like an ocean-trapped blizzard – except in the ship's wake, where, nudged aside, it left a slick runway. So many shades of blue. A peculiar kind of blue, not quite jade and not quite turquoise, but a colour that fell in a deep cleft between. The artist Frances Walker knows this colour and caught it perfectly in her paintings. In 2007 she visited these islands and returned home to capture their scale and breadth in her *Antarctic Suite*, now held at the McManus gallery in Dundee. They are considered her finest work.

The paintings are huge – large sheets of marine ply stuck together in diptychs and triptychs with obvious joins as if to say, *a single painting is not enough for this*. The horizons are tilted or turned down at the edges, following the curve of the Earth. And that Antarctic blue, so perfectly grasped, brighter where sunlight falls, dark and metalled in the shadows of clouds, reveals itself best in the cusps of backlit waves – a colour as biting as a gasp of winter air – and along the shoreline too, at the edges of bergs where porous ice is steeped in liquid blue.

Walker's painting of Elephant Island shows the sea striated in white caps, broken by dark triangular peaks, snow slumped down their sides, summits retreating into cloud. The abrupt coastline marks a stark transition from sheer mountainside to sea and hides no place to land a boat; this is no gentle island of coves and beaches. A thin layer of light on the horizon tells us that nothing else is here; this singular place lives in complete isolation.

We anchored at midnight just off Point Wild, cocooned once again in that eerie blue-tinted half-light, sandwiched between flat sea and low cloud. The island's snow-covered peaks disappeared into clouds, emerging, I imagined, from their tops as yet another set of peaks: islands upon islands.

On a map, an elephant's head stretches out its trunk; Point Wild lies halfway along its top. This tiny piece of rubbled land squeezed between two fat glaciers forms the small promontory on which twenty-two men spent the austral winter of 1916.

Frank Wild was left in charge of the men at Elephant Island as Shackleton sailed a tiny lifeboat 800 miles to the whaling stations of South Georgia. It was a long shot, the navigational equivalent of finding a needle in a haystack. The stamina and sea-faring skill needed for this voyage was Herculean, and Frank Worsley, captain of the *Endurance*, deserves much of the credit, but Frank Wild was no less heroic. Along with the abandoned crewmen, he waited four and a half months for help to arrive when expected within weeks. War had broken out in Europe, and the British, while sympathetic, lacked the resources to lend to Shackleton for the rescue of his men. After several failed attempts, turned back by pack ice, Shackleton made it to Elephant Island with the help of the Chilean navy in a small tugboat named *Yelcho*.

As he stood on the deck of the *Yelcho*, looking towards Elephant Island, Shackleton counted his men waving from the beach. Turning to Worsley at his side, he murmured, 'They are all there, skipper – they are all safe.' To the surprise of the rescuers, Frank Wild and his men stood packed and ready to leave. In a feat of enduring optimism, each morning, if the bay had been clear of ice, Wild had risen, packed his bag and told the men, 'Roll up your sleeping-bags, boys; today, the boss may come.'

At 5.30 a.m., we woke and dressed, donned life-jackets and climbed down rope ladders into the waiting Zodiacs. A cruise ship had booked in to anchor at 9 a.m., so we had to be away before then. We might have been in the Antarctic wilderness, but it was a tightly scheduled wilderness, managed to maintain the impression of emptiness.

The morning mist hung thick, the only hint of colour from the pale steel-blue of ice and the dark jade sea. Bobbing brash dampened the incoming waves as Jordi helmed our Zodiac through the haze to give us a closer look at one of the glaciers. Hearing the creaks and groans of this shifting monster felt thrilling. We watched as large chunks of ice spat out like cannon-shot and fell almost in slow motion to the water below, rippling roller-coaster shockwaves through the sea. We held on for the ride, and when it calmed, Jordi pointed out a huge lump as clear as glass.

'The clearer the ice, the older it is. This must be thousands of years old. Imagine that,' he grinned.

Jordi steered us to the tiny spit of land where Wild and his men had camped. It looked impossibly small. Cemented into the bedrock stood a solitary bust of Luis Pardo, captain of the *Yelcho*. It was an oddity among the crags, nesting penguins and surf, more suited to a marbled museum atrium, though here it likely commanded more attention, misplaced in its savage surrounds. Jordi, a superb photographer himself, often seen on shore trips with a camera lens as long as his arm, gave us plenty of time to take our own snaps, angling the Zodiac to include *Europa* as a backdrop.

'Where did they camp?' I asked.

Jordi pointed to a small space below the cliff. 'It used to be bigger, but there's been a rockfall since then.' The area was barely above the waterline. They must have been swamped in a storm.

It's astonishing what people can step up to when out of options. Twenty-two men crammed beneath a pair of up-turned lifeboats in one of the most inhospitable places on Earth, living off penguins and limpets for four and a half months, not knowing if they'd be rescued. I once spent six weeks in a soggy tent in the Lake District doing fieldwork for my undergraduate dissertation. That had proved difficult enough.

As we returned to the ship, the mist lifted. Ice crystals drifted in the air and refracted shards of rainbows in the sunlight. We'd dawdled a little too long, and as we hauled up our anchor, a sparkling cruise ship trundled in. The passengers at the rails did not return our waves, so Kate and I pulled faces at them and talked of launching a pirate raid for softer toilet roll, chocolate and Wi-Fi.

As we sailed away, a long swell overtook us from the stern, lifting the ship from behind and rolling beneath us. Bill joined me at the helm, looking a little dwarfed in his bright red sailing jacket. We hadn't seen much of him on the voyage; he spent most of his time hanging out with the engineers or hidden away with a book.

'Not much evidence of your global warming here, is there? Still plenty of ice, eh?'

I knew he was doing his best to bait me, and I let out a long sigh. 'You know it's not that simple,' I said. I often felt inept when talking about climate change. The science is complex, and there are no easy soundbites or solutions. 'Didn't you see how much the glaciers had melted on South Georgia? The lines where they used to be were way above where the tops of the glaciers are now.'

'Nah, I didn't go ashore. Turn it to starboard,' he said, seeing me struggle with the helm. The swell from behind had risen and quickened and made steering difficult. I fought with the wheel to stay on course, readjusting with each wave that passed beneath us. My eyes darted back and forth from the compass to the horizon, confused by our shifting direction and the course I needed to steer to correct our drift.

'Climate change is natural, though. It was happening well before we came along,' Bill said.

'But it's never happened this fast before. We've no idea what we're playing with here. Humans can't adapt that quickly. Pretty much all the scientists agree on that.'

A huge wave rolled beneath us and caught the rudder, knocking the wheel out of my hands. Bill grabbed it and straightened us up.

'Do you want me to take over?'

'Yes, please.'

'How do we know for certain it's us causing it, though?' he said.

'There's no doubt any more. Anyway, can we risk being wrong? The consequences are devastating.' I rattled them off – wildfires, floods, hurricanes, typhoons, heat waves, tornadoes, water shortages, famines.

'That's part of life. These things happen anyway.'

'But we're causing them to happen more often. And as usual, it's the rich Western countries inflicting it on the world's poor.'

'Yeah, but what's the answer? Stop everything? Ban all cars? Ban flying? No more fancy sailing trips to Antarctica for you, or anyone else for that matter.'

'I know. You're right. I shouldn't be here at all.' I turned and looked back at our wake as it rose and fell in the swell behind us. Bill had steered us on a steadier course, and I could see the wavering of my attempts zigzagging in the distance.

I told him how I had stopped flying for fifteen years because of climate change. Then all the new budget airlines sprang up and everyone started flying to Europe for weekend city-breaks or shopping trips to New York.

'I felt a bit of a mug, if I'm honest,' I said.

Whether I liked it or not, I was utterly complicit. I didn't have the answers, and, like most people, I often felt paralysed by the choices I had to make day to day.

'We need governments to take it seriously,' I said. 'We've got the technology to make the changes, but they just won't do it.'

'We can't afford to do it. It'll cost too much. People can't just switch to electric cars like that. And even if we did, how would we power them?' Bill asked. 'You don't want nuclear, and wind power is a bloody nonsense. It doesn't exactly blow on demand.' He pointed up at our sails luffing in the breeze, more from the forward motion of our engines than from any wind. 'It's like whaling,' he said. 'People weren't whaling for the hell of it. It was for food. It's what kept people going after the war.'

Except they didn't need whales for food. Most of the time they just used them for fertiliser or animal feed. Scientists have to do years of research to back up their claims, whereas corporations somehow get away with making bold, unsubstantiated statements like *we need it for food*. The fossil-fuel industries are as bad; they've used lobbying organisations to block, resist and sow doubt on the climate-change debate since the science began to emerge. They are adept at 'greenwashing' – using powerful marketing techniques to persuade us of their responsible environmental ethics, when in reality their actions differ substantially from their projected image. And we continue to fill our cars at their petrol stations, herded down a well-trammelled path and consistently nudged in the direction of consumption, because that's what we know. The intensive fishing and agro-industries greenwash us too, touting their heritage as a weapon, yet there is little homely and pastoral about these operations; large-scale agro-business bears as much resemblance to a family-run farm as the giant factory ships did to whaling by indigenous cultures in canoes.

'The bottom line,' Bill said, 'is that you can't have this many people on the planet and a pristine environment. Humans have an impact, and we just have to suck it up. Too many bloody people – that's the real problem. And there's no easy answer to that.'

I looked out ahead of us. A slight pinprick glimmer at the base of the clouds on the far horizon hinted at land. The South Shetland Islands, perhaps? I pulled out the binoculars tucked in my jacket but could see nothing there.

I turned back to Bill. 'I know there are no simple solutions, but I refuse to give up hope.'

That evening, after our last shift, we relaxed in the deck-house. Kate appeared with a bottle of gin. 'G&Ts?' she beamed, filling up our glasses. We toasted to Frank Wild, all of us moved by his story. The courage to be optimistic, to rise each day in the face of bleakness, takes endurance of inconceivable magnitude.

~

The *Southern Soldier* pushes further into the Weddell Sea. Heavy swells and sleet close in around the boat, making it hard to see any distance. Up in the barrel, you shrink into your jacket against the cold but still keep a keen lookout; pack ice can appear out of nowhere and surround the boat within minutes. But you've learned to sense it before you see it: the sudden drop in temperature, the slackening of wind, the smooth seas and deeper silence.

Large icebergs are more of an insidious threat. They often move against the flow of the wind-driven pack ice. Propelled from their roots by deep currents, they follow their own unpredictable path. If one comes your way, the only option is to change course.

A week into your new job, and whales are suddenly scarce – none sighted so far. The crew is listless and bored, the gunner especially ill-tempered. He drinks heavily between his shifts. 'Keep out of his way,' Eck tells you. 'He thinks you've brought us bad luck.'

Between watches, you lie in the warmth of your cabin next to the main engine and flick through the book Ferguson gave you. The chapter titles alone send a shiver through you: 'Land of Ghosts', 'White Darkness', 'Demon Tempests', 'Flying Skulls'. The author, Thomas Henry, describes the Weddell Sea as 'the most treacherous and dismal region on earth'. You frown at the words, but it seems most expeditions here are soon driven back by winds and ice. You read on. 'It is a sea of howling winds, of spectres and portents with frequent mirages, luminous purple clouds and ghostly halos around the sun . . . notorious for its flash freezes . . . spelling disaster for at least three expeditions.'

You know how Shackleton's ship in particular succumbed to the Weddell Sea's treachery. He picked this place to land his party ashore, even though the South Georgia whalers told him the ice was too severe. Henry recounts the tale you know so well: the pack ice piling high around the *Endurance*, shifting and stacking, almost a living, breathing creature, trapping the ship in the Weddell gyre for nearly ten months before finally she was crushed, her crew stranded on the floes. You shudder to imagine. Here, your ship is your life.

In your bunk one night, you sense the engines slow. You hear shouts from the deck and ice grinding against the hull. Then a sudden lurch. The ship's whistle signals all hands.

You rush to pull on your oilskins and boots and head out on deck. The cold hits you first – deep, solid and eerie. The *Soldier* is surrounded by pack ice: bumping, shuffling blocks as far as you can see.

The gunner and first mate hang over the bow rails and point at the hull below.

The second mate shouts across at you from the helm. 'Get down to the fo'c'sle and help Mick.'

You find the engineer stuffing rags into a fist-sized hole in the hull. Water gushes into the boat. Eck is there too.

'She's punctured her hull. Here, help me with these hoses,' Eck shouts. You can hear the panic in his voice. The hoses are in a mess, and you both fumble, trying to untangle them. Curses from Mick rain down on you. It takes too long. The *Soldier* begins to list as seawater floods her bilges. Finally you get the hoses stretched out and feed them up to the deck and out through the gunnels.

'You, boy, come and hold this,' Mick shouts. You have to lean all your weight against the bundle of rags to stem the steady flow of freezing water, and soon you're soaked. You try not to panic.

You hear the pump start up as water laps at your shins. The steady rise begins to slow. Mick disappears to his workshop and returns twenty long minutes later with two small metal plates to fix over the hole – one for the outside, one for the inside, and a bolthole through the middle of each. You ache with cold and can't feel your hands but desperately try to keep the pressure on the leak as the water pours in, runs up your sleeves and down the front of your oilskins, squirting out from both sides of you.

Mick ties a bit of wood to the end of a thin rope and gets you to step back while he pushes it through the gushing hole. Eck, ready on the deck above, fishes out the wood and ties the rope to the bolt fixed through the plate. He signals with two tugs on the rope, and Mick pulls it in until the plate sits square over the outside of the hole. He threads the bolt through the inner plate and tightens it up. It's a smart fix and stems almost all of the water. Mick welds the inner plate in place, stopping the last of the leak. The water, around your ankles now, begins to ebb, but your shivering is uncontrollable.

'Go and get yourself warmed up, boy,' Mick snaps.

The *Soldier* turns around for the two-day journey back to Stromness on South Georgia for repairs.

'At least let's catch some bloody whales on the way,' the gunner says, as you serve him supper. But you notice he avoids eye contact with you.

The weather improves; the sun comes out. You volunteer for extra shifts on lookout. In the clear early morning air, you scour the seas for whales, hoping to turn around the boat's bad luck. The views are spectacular; the deep sapphire seas are speckled with bright icebergs. Then, far out on the horizon, tell-tale misty cones catch your eye: whale spouts! Great tall ones. Blues, perhaps. Blue whales blow tall and narrow, as do fins, though not as high; humpbacks have wide, heart-shaped blows, and sperm whales shoot a tall gush of water into the air like cartoon whales.

'*Hvalblåst!*' you shout, and point just off the starboard bow.

The gunner looks up at you from the helm and punches his fist into the air. 'Full speed ahead!'

With a great belch of smoke from her funnel, the bow lifts high out the water, and the boat wheels around, heading towards the pod; the chase is on. You grip the sides of the barrel, thrilled at the speed, grinning ear to ear.

Men emerge on deck, dishevelled from their bunks, to tend the winches, lines and gun. The steward appears, excited to see the action. Even Mick's head emerges from the skylight to get a look. It takes the *Soldier* more than two hours to close in on the pod. The gunner confirms the tall upright blows of blue whales.

From your elevated view, you look down through clear seas: a family of about fifteen. A few calves cling to their mothers' sides. You've only ever seen dead whales up close before, and you marvel at their great arch-shaped heads, their long lithe bodies. And the colour! You always wondered why blue whales were called blue when their skin is really a pale grey, but from up here, looking down through the water, they glow an irresistible iridescent turquoise, like the colours you see lapping at the edges of growlers and bergs. Sunlight shifts and mottles the blue across their backs. The noise of their breath is so loud and powerful. You blow air out of your cheeks to mimic them, breathe with them, but as you approach, you notice their breath shorten; they surface more often and blow harder. You begin to feel out of breath too.

The gunner hands the wheel to the first mate and runs along the high wooden walkway that joins the bridge and gun platform. He pivots the gun with its pistol grip and follows the pod, singles out a large female, and sets her in his sights. He adjusts his aim with the roll of each wave. The pod panics, swims faster, defecating krill-pink plumes behind them. But they cannot outrun the catcher. Soon they are just off the bow. They become more breathless. The calves struggle to keep pace. You feel their panic in your chest. Suddenly you're willing them on, urging them to escape, desperate for these glorious creatures to live, to not end up under the spiked boots of the flensers on the factory deck.

'Slow speed,' the gunner shouts from the bow as he directs the boat with arm signals, bouncing with excitement. The sonar engineer follows the whale's outline under water and shouts up to the bridge.

'Starboard side – surfacing,' he shouts.

You can see the long flat head of the whale rising, her great powerful body and strong tail working hard. She is immense. The gunner aims ahead of her dorsal fin.

Then nothing. The gun jams.

~

I woke late, emerging on deck from the dark of our cabin, dazzled by cobalt seas. After so many grey days, the world glowed. We were dashing south across the Bransfield Strait towards the Antarctic Peninsula to set our feet on the continent so elusive of early explorers, though we had the advantage of a map and favourable winds at our back. Lucent icebergs surrounded us, but no pack ice troubled our lookouts.

Kate found me out on the bow, well wrapped against the bright cold, my face turned up to the sun, enjoying the scrap of warmth in it.

'We saw a blue whale!' she said, animated and excited. 'It just popped up on the starboard side on our watch this morning, so close!'

I felt sad to have missed it. The magnificent and elusive blue whale, and, as it turned out, the only one sighted on our entire trip. I thought about the story of 52 Blue. At a naval listening station on the Pacific Northwest coast of the US, back in 1989, hydrophones picked up the songs of a whale, characteristic of a baleen whale, most likely a blue. But the frequency of fifty-two hertz was far higher than any blue whale had been heard to sing before. Over fifteen years between August and February, the station followed his ambling tracks off the coastlines of Alaska and Washington State – it was assumed the whale was male, given they sing the loudest songs – though no other whales were ever detected in the vicinity of his calls, and some speculated he might be a hybrid blue and fin, neither fitting in to one community nor the other. He found fame when newspapers reported the story, dubbing 52 Blue the 'loneliest whale in the world', a creature wandering and looking for love, his songs unheard by other whales. He became an emblem, a cause célèbre for the lost, lonely and disaffected outcasts of the world, though he was never seen.

Blue whales are most often sighted alone or occasionally in pairs nowadays. They may shift in and out of pods depending on the time of year and gather to feast on swarms of krill in the summer. Between 325,000 and 360,000 blue whales were killed in the Southern Ocean in the twentieth century. As few as 5,000 remain today. Perhaps they did all once swim in huge pods, but the swarm of factory fleets put an end to that. The oldest blue whales – they live up to a hundred years – might still remember back to the times when they swam together as groups, a vague and distant dream perhaps, a sense of moving in unison, bonded to those around them, familial songs etched into a primal memory. Do they dream of those days when they filled the seas surrounded by their kin?

In the afternoon, I took advantage of the calm and climbed the main mast to the second platform, a tricky clamber requiring upper-body strength and a steely nerve. From the ship's rails, shrouds were strung to just below a platform at the middle of the mast. Horizontal wooden struts fixed between them formed a ladder. Climbing the shrouds took me to just below the platform, and then I had to navigate the futtock shrouds, which stretch up and outwards from the mast to the outer edge of the platform. This part of the climb was my nemesis, and my heart raced, despite being harnessed and clipped on. By the time I reached the second platform, my mouth felt parched from exertion and fear. The climb to the third platform looked more precarious on the narrow, wobbly ladder, so I didn't attempt it; even in calm seas the mast swung like a metronome. I felt in awe of the permanent crew, who moved deftly around the rigging, strong-armed and light-footed.

I sat up on my high perch, legs dangling over the edge, nestled among the complexity of ropes, sails and rigging, the decks below me dotted with tiny people. Cirrus clouds hung in gauzy layers along the horizon, broken by jagged icebergs. I could see land to the southwest, my first sighting of the Great White Continent, ice caps softening all but the highest peaks.

We'd reached the Antarctic Sound, which runs between the head of the peninsula and the Joinville Island group. An archipelago of place names charts the expeditions that first sailed these waters in the nineteenth and early twentieth centuries. In 1838, French explorer Captain Jules-Sébastien-César Dumont d'Urville named Joinville Island after François, Prince of Joinville. D'Urville later had an island named after him too, by Otto Nordenskjöld of the 1901–04 Swedish Antarctic Expedition; he also named James Ross Island after James Clark Ross's expedition of 1839–43. British naval officers feature heavily too: Graham Land, the northern part of the Antarctic Peninsula, was named after one of the First Lords of the Admiralty, and the Bransfield Strait was named for Royal Navy officer Edward Bransfield. Of course, the Argentines and Chileans have different names for many of these places, so it depends whose map you look at.

Among the islands, the sea lay littered with slabs of ice-shelf, broken up into smaller bergs, but most still huge – one carved into a perfect archway high enough to sail our ship through, though the deep sound of splinters and fractures forming within its hulk, accelerated by the warm sun and the gentle swell of the sea, would have deterred anyone from trying such a foolhardy move. Far off, patches of pack ice speckled the sea. When we passed growlers, their wide, plat-formed hems glowed vivid through the shallow waterline, and just a small fragment of their knobbly middles breached the surface like crocodile eyes. From up here, the world seemed expansive, pristine, untrammelled and gorgeously perfect. Only the gaping absence, what we couldn't see, marked its darker industrial history: the whales that didn't surround our ship in curiosity as they once had for early explorers.

I felt the breeze chill my nose and cheeks as it fed the fat bellies of the sails, moulding them into perfect arcs, tugging the neat rings holding them fast them to the shrouds. My gaze shifted nearer: the sail, ripped in the storm before we reached South Georgia, re-rigged, expertly patched, double-stitched and strengthened at the corners; the stays and wires fixing the mast, binding the ship and holding firm in the fiercest storms, the joins all neatly oiled and wrapped in hand-stitched leather covers to protect them from salt corrosion; the complex webbing of ropes, perfectly tied knots and splices; the wooden blocks we'd spent hours sanding down in the deckhouse reeved back into the rigging, amber varnish glinting in the sun. Nothing was left to chance – a single frayed rope in high winds could spell disaster. The *Europa* had been hand-built with love. Hours, weeks and years of care had been spent by crews and volunteers maintaining her, their hearts and souls woven into her fabric, and now it felt like there was a tiny piece of us in her too. Below, I could make out bosun Emma's slow rolling gait as she strolled the decks, running a hand over a sheet to check the tension, re-coiling a rope left untidy. Though everyone appeared tiny from up here, each person moved in their own way; there was a familiarity in their stature, their movements, the cut and colour of their clothes. Bill stood at the helm, and though I could not see his expression, I could tell from the shape of his face that he was grinning. Janke stood beside him in her striped beanie, arms folded, relaxed, every now and again pointing something out in the distance. Klaas leant both elbows on the deckhouse roof, gazing out to the horizon, the breeze flicking around his wild silvery hair. Kate stood with Lex at the stern rails watching birds glide in our wake. Seated on a bench midships, Peter leaned back against the rails, eyes closed and face turned up to the sun, a book spread unread across his knees. And tucked away on the foredeck, behind a strapped-down Zodiac, out of the wind and hidden from all views but above, Heikki lay flat out, arms folded behind his head, soaking up the warmth of the afternoon sun. I felt a wide expanse in my chest, a catch in my throat, pride and love for our ship, our transient family, our pod.

~

The gunner is furious. As you head back to your cabin you hear him shouting, 'Nothing but bad luck since that boy's been aboard.' You feel wretched. You willed the gun to jam, and it did.

Late that evening, the *Soldier* arrives in Stromness. She is lifted into the dry dock, and work begins immediately, continuing through the night, the gunner not wanting to waste a single day he could be out fishing.

By early the following morning, the hull is repaired, but no fault is found with the gun.

The *Soldier* heads south again, but you're no longer asked to be on lookout; now you work in the galley and on cleaning duties. Half a day out of Stromness and you hear Eck's shout, '*Hvalblåst!*' You feel the rise of the bow as the *Soldier* surges forward at full speed. You rush out on deck, ready to help, but you're shoved aside, told to keep well out of the way, and all you can do is watch.

It's another pod of blues: a huge one, maybe fifty or more. The radio operator sends word to the factory ship and Leith Harbour to alert the other catchers. The whales are easy pickings, and the gunner singles out the biggest female and fires his first shot. The steel-forged harpoon, weighing in at 200 pounds – the weight of a strong sturdy man – buries itself deep in her side. Four steel barbs flick out and lodge against the inside of her rib cage to fix it in place. The grenade, fused to explode three seconds after the gun is fired, detonates in a dull explosion as the whale rolls forward. She jerks violently, lumps of flesh landing in the water around her. 'Stop engines,' shouts the gunner. Blood gushes from her wound, but the whale is not killed, and she dives. For a moment, there is silence, just the noise of the taut nylon rope birling out from the locker below. The line runs up through the boat's mast that bends and takes the strain like a fisherman's rod. Finally, the line slackens, and the gunner signals the winch man to wind it in. They play the whale like a caught fish: the line is run and winched, run and winched, but, unlike a fish, the whale needs to breathe air, and her lungs are filling with blood. She surfaces, thrashing her tail, fighting the line, but soon she slows and tires. The men are disappointed she doesn't show the traditional chimney of fire – the spout of blood that accompanies the death of most whales. But she is not dead. The fight goes out of her, and she turns onto her side, rolling her blowhole above the waterline each time she needs to take a breath, her blood tainting the sea a vivid scarlet.

She is hauled alongside, barely alive, two thirds the length of the catcher boat, and now she watches as they puncture her with bamboo poles and fill her belly full of compressed air to keep her body afloat. Her tail flukes are sliced off and discarded. Notches are cut into the stump of her tail – three notches for catcher number three – to mark her as theirs, ensuring they get their due bonus.

The mate comes over and hands you a long spike of metal with a flag and a wireless transmitter on the top to guide in the boats collecting her for the factory. 'Here, lad, put this in its side. You'll need to give it a good shove so it doesn't fall over.'

You lean out over the rails looking for a place to put it. 'Just there,' the mate tells you, pointing at her flank. As you're about to plunge the spike into her side, she rolls over and looks you in the eye. The flag drops from your hand and clatters to the deck. The mate curses, grabs the spike and plunges it in for you.

Eck, still up the barrel, has kept track of the rest of the pod. The whale is cast off, left to a slow death, petrels and albatross gathering to peck at her flesh. But just as the *Soldier* turns away, you see it, swimming up to her side – a young calf, nudging in to her inflated belly.

The hunt resumes, and the rest of the fleet soon joins in. The killing lasts a full two days, decimating the rest of the pod.

~

At eight that evening, though as bright as day, we motored through the Antarctic Sound on mirrored seas. Penguins porpoised in small clans through the ice-strewn waters. A lone humpback passed us travelling in the opposite direction and gave a show of his glossy flukes. We anchored just off Brown Bluff – a tuya volcano, formed when lava erupts through thick ice, cools quickly and piles up into a steep-sided, flat-topped heap. The buff-coloured rock face plummeted to a narrow beach of smooth black pebbles, and glaciers ran down either side to the tideline. Ferried ashore in the Zodiacs, we gathered for a group photograph surrounded by penguins, our feet planted on Antarctic soil: the final and seventh continent tick-boxed for those counting.

Lex led us up the side of the volcano, indicating he had a treat in store: a cliff face of rare pillow lavas – volcanic rock formed from eruptions underwater where lava oozes out between cracks in the ocean floor like gobs of toothpaste. Pillow lavas cool quickly on the outside and more slowly inside, creating halos of rock, visible when they are split apart. I'd seen plenty of these in textbooks but never in real life. It was a rare treat for a rock geek like me.

From our high vantage point, we looked across the bay to our small ship, timeless and tethered among the icebergs, her sails gloriously rucked on her yards against a pale backdrop of ice and polar skies, the only movement from penguins and the gentle drift of growlers.

Towards 10 p.m., we walked back down to the shore along the edge of the glacier, picking through large boulders and scree. Rocks balanced like mushroom caps on the ice-stalks they'd insulated beneath them. Amid this strange landscape we watched in silence as a full moon rose, bright in the pale sunset. We'd sailed from Montevideo on the full moon, and now, one full lunar month later, we were on the most extreme and beautiful continent in the world. I felt the need to take off my boots and socks. As I stood in my bare feet, connecting to this strange, wild, dreamy and precarious place, the tears streamed down my face.

Antarctica – the furthest *away* I could go. A place, I'd thought, that cared not a jot for the folly of humanity, where only nature dictated the narrative, and where deep geological time quietly groaned at its own pace. Yet even here felt fleeting, just one breath in time; even this would change – was already changing: the plastics, the warming, the exploitation and the gaping absence of all that had already been ripped from her belly.

I cried for the mothers too, the ones who'd lost their sons to this place, who had sent them away in good faith and never saw them return. I couldn't imagine being so brave.

I wondered if it was coincidence that so many of us on our journey were grieving from recent loss, perhaps drawn to the still places in the face of relentless change, just wanting the world to stop so we could catch our breath. Each loss we suffer – of our parents, our friends, our partners – accumulates. But environmental grief is different: each generation inherits a denuded and less authentic version of the Earth, so change can almost go unnoticed. Only by looking back in time can we make any real sense of the scale of what has been lost. But this hindsight costs us the keenest grief of all.

Our allocated time on the continent was up, and the guides were anxious to get us back to the ship. As we climbed into the Zodiacs, the moon slung her bright streak across the still seas. Shades of apricot, rose, amber and gold splashed lavishly across the water, across the low clouds and pale icebergs. A clear blue still clung to the sky high above us. The twilight hues hung for hours as sunset spliced into sunrise in a queer silence and our ship slipped through glassy waters. I stayed out on the stern deck, silent until morning, watching Antarctica ebb in our wake, unable to take my eyes from this vanishing world.

6

El Fin del Mundo

After our landing on the Antarctic Peninsula, we crossed
back over the Bransfield Strait to the westerly end of the South
Shetland Islands, first visiting a giant cinder cone the colour
of paprika with splashes of sulphurous turmeric. As we
crested the high crater rim, we looked down to find a smaller
cone within. Standing on the edge, we had a fisheye-lens
view right around the island: budgerigar-blue seas lapped at
its feet under a sky full of lenticular clouds. It was a landscape Dali would have been proud to envisage.

We moved on to Greenwich Island, beaching the Zodiacs on the isthmus at Fort Point, a skyscraper-tall pinnacle
of rock blotted by ochre-red guano and raucous gentoo
and chinstrap penguins nesting on its flanks. As we
walked, stepping-stone-sized pebbles rang hollow beneath
us. Each tumbled smooth by waves, the pebbles nestled
together in a perfect mosaic, uniform and dull when dry,
but gleaming on the wet shore: jet-black basalt, speckled
grey granite and greeny gabbro sprinkled with chunks of
translucent ice washed ashore. It was testament to the
pent-up energy in these seas – the bigger the pebbles on a
beach, the fiercer the storms that shaped them. I could

only imagine the monumental surf that had sculpted those stones.

At the land end of the isthmus, a wide glacier front towered above the tideline, and we sneaked as close to its edge as we dared, its roughened and precarious front liable to drop tons of ice into the sea at any time. It felt thrilling to be so close, like tiptoeing past a sleeping dragon, but we might never again see such a huge glacier snout up close. The top stretched almost half a mile along the shore, domed and featureless, but at its front, contorted barcode bands of snow and rockfall catalogued the glacier's life as it had groaned its way across the island.

On the adjacent beach we found debris from an old sealing boat, a wooden mast weathered smooth and pale, and, nearby, a modern-day plastic fender lost from a ship. Even these remote islands were not immune to flotsam and jetsam.

As we reboarded *Europa*, a humpback whale and her calf drifted into the bay. We'd spotted few humpbacks on our trip and flocked to the bow rails to see them, cameras glued to our faces. She swam right to us, sticking out her nose for a better view, calf close by her side.

Humpbacks are arguably the most beautiful of the whales – shorter, but rounder and plumper than the rocket-sleek fins and blues. And such long elegant pectoral fins, laced in barnacles. Wafting through the seas, the merest undulation of the spine turns them; the slightest flick of the tail gathers speed. They can be showy too, diving in a slow roll of dripping flukes or leaping, testing the gravity of their bulk in the thinness of the air, slapping down palm-flat fins then rolling just below the surface to look up into the bright blue above.

The whalers hated killing humpbacks – like shooting puppies, they said. So trusting and curious, they would swim right up to the catcher boats. They were the first whales to be brought to the brink of extinction in Antarctic waters, their numbers plummeting to almost nothing around South Georgia by 1914, just a decade after the start of whaling there. Their rapid disappearance began to ring alarm bells with the early conservation pioneers.

Surprisingly soon into the Antarctic whaling bonanza, a prominent champion for the whales emerged: Sidney Harmer, keeper of zoology and eventual director of the British Museum of Natural History. Born in 1862, Harmer studied at University College London and was often seen riding around on his penny-farthing. Later, as an academic fellow and tutor at Cambridge, he became known for his industry, patience and accuracy in observation, and his precision in zoological recording. He abhorred any hurried clutching at results. In 1909, aged forty-seven, he took up his post at the British Museum, where he became known for his prolific research, tact and self-effacing nature. His later appointment as director was made after a board member remarked that 'nobody could possibly quarrel with Harmer'. It was at the museum that his interests turned to cetaceans; he organised coastguards around Britain to report any whales or dolphins stranded on their shores. This scheme elevated the British Museum's collection of whales to be among the best in the world and rapidly increased our knowledge of marine mammals and their seasonal movements around the British coastline.

Harmer took on the anti-whaling cause in 1908, insisting that an extermination was underway and, moreover, unforgivable. He'd been alerted to the potential dangers of unrestricted whaling by a letter from a Norwegian engineer expressing concerns about the reckless extravagance of the whaling companies. At the time, whales were stripped of their blubber and the remains discarded, even though the meat and bones contained almost half the oil. The waters around shore-based stations swam thigh-deep in a swill of rotting flesh, whales so abundant the industry could afford such profligacy.

Harmer began to examine the catch data for South Georgia and was the first to plot the plummeting graph of the humpbacks' demise, though he had no proof to support his theory that it had been caused by whaling. Without clear evidence, his claims fell on the deaf ears of the whaling companies' executives – and of the British Colonial Office – who were busy making grand profits and stood emphatic in the unsubstantiated view that the Antarctic held an inexhaustible supply of whales; the industry only had to make money, and that was easy, especially when allowed unfettered access to an abundant untapped resource. And it was an international problem: Britain may have controlled the shore stations, but factory ships came under no jurisdiction.

As long ago as 1833, British economist William Forster Lloyd described how unregulated access to a shared resource can lead to individuals acting in their own self-interest and exploiting the resource to depletion. The concept later became known as 'The Tragedy of the Commons', after the typical overgrazing that occurs on common land. The idea is key to the climate-change debate, with the *But what about China?* argument regularly touted as an excuse for our own nations' inaction. Only societies focused on sustainable subsistence as opposed to wealth accumulation have ever avoided this trap.

The International Whaling Commission was established in 1946, but, unwilling to upset the cash-cow of industry, the quotas they set proved ridiculously high. Rumours circulated among the whalers that the Russians and Japanese frequently underreported their catches anyway, pushing everyone to bend the rules a little. Pregnant females, nursing mothers and short whales were pretty much all fair game – and besides, in a rough sea, mistakes were so easy to make.

The whaling companies had the ear of the government, could afford (by this point) to pay for the ear of the government. *Britain needs margarine* was their mantra. The scientists were scuppered – so little was known about the whales in terms of stocks, reproduction rates and migration patterns – and the lessons of the Arctic, where whale stocks were already depleted, had not been learned.

Harmer doggedly pressed for more research into the southern whale populations throughout his career, and though he never visited the Antarctic, he became instrumental in setting up the early Discovery Investigations of the 1920s. Keen to disassociate from the industry, which by this time had amassed a vast amount of information about whales, Harmer eschewed the whalers, so the scientists had to start from scratch. The early investigations were unfruitful and became the laughing stock of the industry. Vast amounts of money were poured into the scientific programme with little to show for it, and only when the scientists became regulars on the flensing platforms of the factory ships and learned the trade first-hand did they begin to understand the science. But then, keen to fit in with their hosts, the scientists' sympathies turned towards the whalers.

It wasn't until the 1960s that the Discovery Investigations got a handle on the data. Finally, they had incontrovertible evidence in support of their theories. But by that time, whale stocks were already so low the whaling fleets were no longer financially viable. The industry had already packed up and moved on. This story of too little, too late echoes prophetically with climate scientists today.

It took until 1986 for the International Whaling Commission to finally issue a moratorium on commercial whaling – fourteen years after it had first been proposed, seventy-eight years after Harmer first sounded the alarm. A loophole, however, allowed countries to issue their own licences to kill whales, ironically for scientific purposes. The following year, Japan issued licences to its own newly formed Institute of Cetacean Research.

In 1994, the International Whaling Commission established the Southern Ocean Whale Sanctuary surrounding the Antarctic continent, prohibiting all whaling within its boundaries. The Sanctuary was recognised by all members, except Japan, which continued with its Antarctic programme. By then, Japanese whaling required heavy subsidies. In 2011, US$29 million of the post-earthquake and tsunami reconstruction budget was diverted to provide security for the Japanese whaling fleet in Antarctica against the growing threat of environmental activists. The activists were Sea Shepherd, under the leadership of Paul Watson.

As we sailed away from Greenwich Island, the mother humpback and her calf followed us at a distance then turned away to explore the shoreline. I wondered what kind of men could kill such gentle creatures, what mindset it took to inflict such slaughter on something so thrillingly beautiful.

We cannot repopulate the oceans with whales and restore the ecosystems that matured around them, in the same way that we cannot replant rainforests that took millions of years to evolve only to be cut down for palm oil or beef grazing for burger conglomerates. We cannot undo these mistakes.

~

The next few weeks are relentless, with the *Soldier*'s fortunes turned around and whales in good supply again. The curse of your bad luck seems to have lifted, but you keep your head down anyway, get on with the job and hide away in your bunk when off duty. Whenever whales are sighted, you volunteer to man the lines in the locker below the gun so you don't have to be up on deck. The crew is happy for you to do it: it's one of the most dangerous jobs on the boat, making sure the lines stay untangled and run freely whenever a whale is caught, re-coiling them afterwards. You have to keep your wits about you. Many a man has had his leg caught in a line with the full weight of a whale on the other end, and if it should snap, the line will whip back like a scythe. But still, you prefer it to the slaughter up on deck.

In early February, you're anchored in a bay off King George Island in the South Shetland Islands, sheltering from a fierce storm. You volunteer for night-time anchor watch, staying awake while the rest of the crew sleeps, keeping a check on your position just in case the boat begins drifting. Every fifteen minutes, you take bearings to landmarks on and around the island. By the early hours of the morning, the storm abates, and an eerie calm descends. These are the moments you love the most, where you can enjoy the quiet breadth of the place in solitude.

On the port side, a whale blow close by catches your eye, a wide heart-shaped puff of mist: a humpback. It's your first encounter with a live humpback – up until now, you've only seen them on the factory deck being sliced and diced for the boilers. It nears the boat and surfaces for a closer look, angling its eye along the length of the hull. A male, you think. He lingers for twenty minutes or so, and you watch mesmerised by the graceful way he moves, slow and sedate, turning and exploring the hull. Then he turns away, heading east along the shore, rolling over, slapping a great flipper down onto the surface and releasing a loud blow as he departs. Minutes later, the gunner emerges on deck, still hooking his braces over his shoulders, tucking in his thick woollen jumper.

'Did I hear a whale?' he asks, looking around.

In your panic, you point west, stuttering words about a humpback. The gunner sounds the whistle to call all hands on deck – he won't miss a single opportunity. He gets out his binoculars and scours the western horizon.

'Why the hell didn't you call us?' he snaps. 'Go and make coffee.'

The crew emerges, the engines are fired up and the *Soldier* heads west, searching for the humpback, but he is not found.

The following day, news reaches the *Soldier* via the factory ship that King George VI, King of the United Kingdom, has died and Queen Elizabeth II has taken his place as monarch. The gunner issues a tot of rum to the British crew to welcome their new queen. It's the first drink you've had since joining the *Soldier*, and the burning around your gums and warmth in your belly brings a fleeting glow to your mood.

At the beginning of March, word comes from the *Southern Venturer* that the whaling season will end in less than a week – nearly a month early. The Southern Ocean fleet quota of 16,000 blue whale units has been reached. You feel a leap of excitement; you're going home! You've barely dared to think about it until now. The rest of the crew is downcast; the *Soldier* is still well below its annual catch average, and the *Venturer* is a long way off achieving her oil target – and is unlikely to reach it now. Wages will be poor this year. The other factory ships must have fared better, exceeding their own targets, while the *Venturer* is left short. You hear the English factory ship, *Balaena*, is already heading home with 180,000 barrels in her tanks. She fishes further east and has an on-board helicopter used for spotting whales from the air.

The men double down, one last push to try to meet the factory target before the season officially ends. On the *Soldier*, the crew scours the seas, killing every last whale it can find, the gunner flexing the rules on what he is allowed to take. You work around the clock, every man pulling together. A small victory is won as the factory makes its meal target, but it's still well short of oil, on which the men's bonuses are based.

On 12 March, the whaling season officially ends. A telegram arrives on the *Venturer* from the Salvesen head office. Like a parent admonishing a wayward child, the bosses, from the comfort of their smart Edinburgh offices, express disappointment in the men, dissatisfied with this year's catch results. The *Southern Venturer* and her sister ship, the *Southern Harvester*, are neck and neck with nearly 2,000 whales apiece, but it's not enough for the bosses.

The *Soldier* brings in the last whale of the season, and the gunner boards the factory, stepping off his catcher for the first time in months. He gets a row from the whaling inspector for all his infractions over the season: the short whales, the pregnant whales, the nursing mothers, the whales brought in after their processing deadline, but he waves away the inspector's concerns with a flap of his hand. He does what he needs to do, and he knows the inspector's threats lack any real bite.

With the last whale processed and down the hatches, the fleet turns back towards South Georgia. The factory men swarm out onto the deck, armed with axes and crowbars for the last job of the season – pulling up the plan deck. They set to work with an extra fury, venting a mix of frustration at this year's low wages and the excitement of heading home. Some, the ones with more sag to their shoulders, have agreed to overwinter in South Georgia for the seventy-five per cent pay increase, but not you. You just want to get home.

The stinking timbers are cast overboard, a swathe of jetsam bobbing in the ship's wake, the real teak deck revealed underneath, grubby and stained from the drip of blood, but almost white once scrubbed clean. The ship is scoured and scraped top to bottom with caustic soda, steam jets and boiling water, the men working ferociously, scrubbing out every damn spot of blood and flesh, every reminder of the slaughter and butchery that has taken place here. Even some of the paint is stripped away under this furious treatment. Below decks, the boilers are cooked up for the last time, but now with fresh water. The tank-gangs go down to clean out the fuel oil, ready to ship home their cargo of whale oil from South Georgia. Even just a tiny drop of fuel oil can contaminate the precious whale oil. It's a horrible job, and dangerous too. On the *Soldier*, you hear a whaler has died in the factory's tanks, overcome by fumes in the confined space. It was his last voyage before retirement and, keen to top up his wages, he'd volunteered for the job as it carried an extra bonus. You knew him; he'd been kind to you. Work on the factory pauses for an hour as he is buried at sea.

Finally the factory ship is clean. The men ditch their working clothes overboard too – the smell would never have come out – and buy new ones from the slop-chest. The weather turns colder, the ship sailing through constant storms and dark skies. You've had your fill of the freezing dark. When you reach home in Scotland, it will be spring.

~

From the beach we ran together, Heikki leading the charge, a long line of us crashing into the icy water, dunking down, surfacing to shrill headaches, then dashing back to our narrow steaming pool that paralleled the shore, where cosy as lukewarm tea we lay top-to-tail nestled down into its dark exfoliating cinder. We were on Deception island in the South Shetland Islands, a horseshoe caldera nine miles in diameter, entered through Neptune's Bellows, where ships suck in their sides to pass into the calm of its natural harbour. It was here that one of the Salvesen whale catchers, the *Southern Hunter*, ran aground on the rocks in 1956 as she steamed into the entrance.

An active volcano, Deception Island lies snow-free most of the year, its underbelly warmed by hydrothermal vents from the sea floor. In the early twentieth century, the heat could take the paint from ships' hulls and melt anchors spiked into its floor, though, for now, it has cooled a little.

We'd been dropped at Pendulum Cove, swimsuits on beneath our winter gear, in the hope of finding a perfect bathing spot. At high tide, warm water percolates up through the beach, stranding cooked krill on the tideline and forming steaming hot pools. We were lucky enough to find one the perfect size and temperature to fit our entire crew. First, we'd explored the tangled and burnt remains of a Chilean research station, mangled and half buried in ash during an eruption in 1967. Before landing, we'd had the safety talk: if the island were to erupt, the ship would exit the harbour first, and we should walk to the outside shoreline to meet it. I looked up at the steep cliffs forming the caldera rim. I didn't much fancy our chances of getting out in a hurry, but the last eruption had been in 1970 so I figured we'd be okay.

We lay as long as we could, running between our steaming pool and the cold sea. It was delicious and the warmest I'd felt since leaving Montevideo. But as the receding tide depleted the cooling seawater from our pool, we felt wafts of hotter and hotter water rise beneath our pink bottoms. We soon looked like cooked krill too and reluctantly dragged ourselves from our bath. Lex dowsed us in buckets of hot water to wash the cinder from our bodies. Back on the ship, we felt vital and invigorated, our skin tingling for the rest of the day.

It was the last stop on our voyage before heading for home across the notorious Drake Passage, a strip of ocean connecting the South Shetland Islands with Cape Horn and the meeting point for the Atlantic and Pacific oceans. The 500-mile crossing has a fierce reputation. Westerly winds squeeze spiralling storm after storm through its narrowed gap, building swells of ten metres or more. A weather window had opened, and the permanent crew seemed antsy, ready to get going and make the most of it: they'd seen 'the Drake' at its worst.

As we weighed anchor the following morning under grim skies, the choppy seas did not look promising, but the weather calmed as we sailed north and we experienced the rarely lulled 'Drake's Lake', polished perfect and slow.

Midway, I stood leaning on the bow railings in the lilac evening light as we chugged north under motor.

Fraser the engineer, gruff and dishevelled in his overalls, in an old biker kind of way, joined me, drawing on his roll-up.

'Alright?'

I nodded. 'You?'

'Grand. Pleased we're not having to battle the storms this time.'

'You been in many storms here?' I ask.

'Oh fuck aye. I've been across here a few times now, but never seen it as calm as this. We're lucky. It'll just about use up the last of our fuel, though.'

'Have we been through a lot?'

'You don't wanna know,' he laughed.

I let out a long sigh. I'd thought sailing would be a more 'eco-friendly' way to travel. I never seemed to get it right.

Sailing north across the polar front, where sea temperatures rose sharply, we began to shed our layers, our bodies feeling less corseted without the wrap of thick fleeces and jackets. The mood became a little subdued, folk pensive about the transition back to their usual lives. Many had taken hard-earned sabbaticals after years of graft, and some were re-evaluating, though we were all looking forward to seeing our families again. Down in the cabins, we fished out our bags and began to empty lockers, packing away our sea lives.

By the time we sighted Cape Horn, the evening sun speared through clouds, igniting patches of sea. The notorious Cape bumped out of the calm off our port side, fierce as a dull day at the municipal pool. While relieved to be across the Drake, I couldn't help feeling a little disappointed at missing out on its savage reputation, though I suspect it would have scared me silly. But as we motored along, a pod of dusky dolphins, perhaps twenty or so, streaked white down their sides, rode lithe on our bow, quickening and darting about the hull, revealing the true clarity of the water that had, until now, seemed dingy and opaque. They needed little effort to keep up with our lumbering six knots and quickly bored of us, slipping off one by one to find better entertainment.

On our last watch that evening, 8 p.m. to midnight, on the austral summer solstice, the skies cleared, the stars came out, and the Milky Way splashed its band of subtle colours over our heads. We dropped anchor at the mouth of the Beagle Channel, and a few of us sat out on deck to relish the cool of the night.

'So what's on your bucket lists next?' Kate asked.

'Our list seems to get longer each year,' Anna said. She and her husband Mike were one of the few couples on board. They were life enthusiasts, living at full pelt. 'We're travelling through Patagonia after this. Antarctica was our seventh continent. Part of the reason we're here, really.' Throughout through the trip, they'd made sure not to miss a single thing, Anna's voice often heard shouting, 'Mike, Mike, take my picture,' as she posed in front of some glacier or elephant seal.

Kate was heading to Australia to see old friends and then on to Galapagos, Peter wanted to take his wife to the States on a campervan road trip, and Heikki was planning to travel through Europe on his motorbike.

All this dashing about. For people who cared so much for the environment, we were doing a damn good job of accelerating its demise.

'What about you, Sandy?' Heikki asked. 'What's next on your list?'

'I'm not sure yet.' I looked up at the still unfamiliar stars. 'I have to make sense of this trip first. There are lots of places I'd *like* to go, but I've spent too much of my life travelling. Perhaps it's time to learn to love staying at home.'

'Shooting star!' Heikki jerked his arm up to point north. We turned to see a long streak of light arc through the sky and burn out.

'Make a wish!' said Kate, and we sat in silence, mulling our desires. What did I wish for? I don't remember. I hate wishes; they either seem too trivial or too grand.

~

The factory and fleet arrive in South Georgia to the smoke and stench of Leith Harbour. Even to the desensitised noses of the factory men, the place reeks. The *Southern Soldier* ties up alongside the line of catchers stretched out across the bay, a row of identical scruffy boats. At the end of the season, they are battered and weather-worn, scabbed with rust and peeling paint. The crews work frantically – the sooner you can strip out the catchers and lay them up for the winter, the sooner everyone can leave for home.

The first thing you do ashore is to make your way to the mail room in the main office, hoping there will be letters waiting for you. You've had no news from home all season, with ships delayed and rerouted and then your transfer to the *Soldier*. You queue alongside other men as the sleet falls, but when you reach the front of the line, there's nothing for you. You ask the manager to check again, and he does, but there are no letters from home. A nagging feeling grows in your belly: worry for your family, wondering if something might have happened while you've been away. The wretched pain of Nana Lina's death last year still gnaws at you, the hurt of not knowing, of not being a part of the family's grieving. Maybe they are still upset with you. Maybe they don't want you home. You shake it off.

Back on the *Soldier*, Eck finds you in the cabin packing up your things.

'Dinnae bother with that just yet,' he tells you. 'We'll not be moving into the barracks until the *Venturer* leaves.'

You ask him what he means. You thought you'd be leaving with the *Venturer*.

'We always go home on the *Southern Opal*. We've another month here first. The *Soldier* is kept running longer than the other catchers so she can shuttle gear and men over to the dry docks and repair shops in Stromness. We'll strip her out next week and move in to the barracks. Did they not tell you that?'

You slump down on your bunk, head in your hands. Another month. It seems like a lifetime away, and then a month's travel home on the *Opal* after that. Two months before you get home, two whole months of not knowing what's happened while you've been away.

There is nothing for it but to pitch in to help strip out the other catchers, but the bitter disappointment brings an added weight to your mood. Men rush about you, eager to load up and get going. Whale lines are discarded, new ones used each season, and the rest of the equipment – harpoons, grenades, gunpowder, air pumps, sextants, binoculars, chronometers – transferred and piled into huge heaps on the factory deck. The fuel and water are pumped out of the catchers' tanks, and all that's left are the harpoon guns; the gunners tend them with love and oil, wrap them in thick greased hessian and canvas to protect them against the brutal cold and damp of the southern winter. They give them a gentle pat before leaving. Each catcher will be painted and overhauled during the winter, bright and fresh as a brand new bath toy ready for the return of her crews the following spring.

The work of loading the *Venturer* goes on for a full week. Men slide about on the filth of the footpaths, passing cargoes hand to hand, the thousands of meal sacks to be stacked in the *Venturer's* hold. You join the chain of men transferring the surplus stores from the factory ship to the shore station for the overwinter crew. An hour in, and your hands are numb with cold. As the man next to you passes over a crate of dried fish, you slip, dropping the crate and falling over into the cold mud, soaking your trousers and jacket, smearing filth across your face. The manager curses at you and doesn't let you go to get cleaned up. You have to work the rest of the day in your muddy clothes.

That evening Eck persuades you to go along to the kino. They are showing *The Three Musketeers*.

'You can't mope about in your bunk reading your books every night,' he says. You decide to give it a go and make your way over. The building, domed like an aircraft hangar, is packed with men in a fug of smoke. The film hasn't started, but already there is nowhere to sit. You stand at the back by the door, but the cold air whistles in as a storm kicks up outside, rattling across the roof.

The film stars Gene Kelly and Lana Turner, who causes the men to shout and leer each time she's in a scene. It's been a long while since they've seen a woman.

Halfway through, the lights go out and the film grinds to a halt. The generator has failed. The kino is plunged into darkness, the only light from the glow of the men's cigarettes. You don't bother to wait for the generator to be fixed and make your way back to the *Soldier*, hunching in to the cold, hanging on carefully as you board, sliding your way across her icy decks.

The dull work of loading up the *Venturer* is brightened briefly by a trip to St Andrew's Bay. She is to take home king penguins for Edinburgh Zoo, and the *Soldier* is packed off to collect them. Penguins are the international currency of zoos and in great demand. They are traded for other animals: zebras, camels and emus.

You land the small lifeboat on a steep shingle beach, the sky streaked a washed-out grey against dark mountains. The sea is bottle-glass clear, pebbles gleaming beneath the cold surf, and rafts of penguins fling themselves to shore, landing slick and black-backed onto the wet shingle.

You've seen plenty of penguins in the last few years, but never so many in one place: the noise is overwhelming, each penguin tipping back its head, raising an orange throat to the sky and shrieking. Weaving in and out of the din, lumbering adolescent penguins in fluffy tan overcoats cheep like sparrows. The colony is vast and fills the entire length of the beach, packed like a sunny day on the Portobello shore – penguins promenading, skirting around the dozing seals, some resting, balanced on their heels.

Eck points to a penguin with a gaping wound in its belly, a bloodied snowy sheathbill pecking at its insides. He laughs and makes some crude remark. The penguin stands motionless, watching.

Catching the penguins is not as easy as you thought. While they are quite tame, they are also strong and, once caught, they explode in your arms, flapping violently and pecking at you with their keen beaks. It's hard work but a good diversion, and you sail back to Leith Harbour that evening in a better mood, your cargo of indignant birds flapping around your feet. The chippy builds a pen for them on the *Venturer*'s deck while men fish from the shore for rock cod, the waters of the bay thick with them, the hooks not even needing bait, making good fisherman of even the most impatient men. Soon they have heaps of fish, gutted and crated for the factory's freezers – enough for the penguins and more besides for the galley.

The men leaving on the *Venturer* board with their belongings to the now overcrowded cabins of the factory, searching for any free spot: storerooms, the doctor's waiting room, even the offices are commandeered for men to bed down for the voyage home.

Finally, the *Southern Venturer* leaves Leith Harbour on 23 March 1952, her cargo logged in the consignment book:

- 119,006 barrels of whale oil
- 25,526 barrels of sperm whale oil
- 2,185 tons of dehydrated meal
- 172 tons of whale liver meal
- 6,160 gallons of whale liver oil
- 25 pounds of Ambergris
- 600 pituitary glands
- 49 king penguins

You stand quayside to wave her off. It's late afternoon, and she sails on the high spring tide. Your old cabin-mates shout down from the rails and jeer. It's hard to see them go. She sounds her horn as she exits the harbour, and then she is gone. The keen wind blasts cold down your collar, the sleet thickens to snow and the darkness draws in. The station is quiet and eerie, suddenly devoid of life. You trudge back to your newly assigned cabin in the barracks.

~

We woke to a glorious morning. To our west, sunshine and feathered clouds grazed the snow-peaked Cordillera

Darwin – the tail-tip of the Andes. The rocky shores of the Beagle Channel reminded me of Scotland's west coast and how it falls ragged into the sea. I felt my first hankering for home. I'd kept it locked up, safe in the back of my mind until now. From within the blue and white of Antarctica, home had felt too distant and unreachable. Over the years, I've learned to compartmentalise my life. When G has been at rock bottom and I've felt desperate for him, I've still gone into work and not just put a smile on my face, but actually enjoyed my day. It makes me feel callous, but it's also a survival tactic. It's the same kind of duality needed to be utterly in love with the rich diversity of our planet while knowing the scale of threat it's under.

I stood on the deck and breathed in the smell of seaweed-strewn beaches, land – and trees! Our first sight of trees since we'd left Montevideo six weeks ago. The texture and greenness of it all felt almost cluttered and intrusive.

The Beagle Channel slices through the islands of Tierra del Fuego and, at its eastern end, splits a chunk of Argentina, with Ushuaia as its main town, from the Chilean islands to the south. At 9 a.m., a pilot boarded to ensure we didn't stray into Chilean territory as we made our way up the channel. He'd brought his teenage daughter with him – it was clearly a rare treat to be on our beautiful ship after the drudgery of guiding cargo vessels and tankers. Our crew beamed with pride as they showed her off to the visitors.

Sailing the channel towards Ushuaia took all morning and most of the afternoon. As the sun stretched over our heads, a buffet lunch was brought out on deck. We'd filled our plates and sat down to eat when our phones began to chime, reconnecting us to the outside world, our attention snatched from the scenery, from each other, sucked into the tiny screens as we worried, for the first time, what we might have missed. It was Wednesday. I couldn't even remember the last time I'd thought about what day of the week it was.

I phoned home. It would be mid-morning – three hours behind.

G answered, and I could feel the relief in his voice as he heard mine.

'I'm alive! I made it!' I said, but the words caught a little in my throat. 'How are you? Are you all okay? How are the kids?'

'I'm fine. We're all fine. I'm so happy to hear your voice. The kids are both here. I'll put you on speaker.'

'Hello, Mum!' they chorused. 'We've missed you.'

'I've missed you too – so much.' That catch in my throat again. 'I can't wait to see you all. I've so much to tell you!'

I looked around to see my friends smiling into their phones as they too reconnected with loved ones, our families seeping back into our lives.

Ushuaia, el fin del mundo – the end of the world – the most southerly town on the planet, came into view, sprawled across the foothills, lacking planning or grace, cookie-cut from the pine forests and backed by formidable snowy peaks. I could see tiny cars moving along its streets and felt a jolt of surprise as the mundane world flicked back into focus.

We nudged into port, docking alongside a couple of cruise ships. Immigration officials checked and stamped our passports, and fresh salad was delivered dockside for our supper. We had one last night on board, but that evening we would step ashore together and do what sailors do in port – head to the nearest bar.

On the dock, I found my sea-legs unsteady and felt a little queasy with the solidity of it all. Ushuaia, wide-streeted and eclectic, mostly accommodates people passing through to

Antarctica or Patagonia. Its southerly maritime climate means even in summer it's often dreich and chilly. It was reminiscent of small backwater Alaskan towns, and I almost expected to see a moose walking down the main street. But there were plenty of rowdy bars for those returning from the wilds.

The crew knew just the place – hot, steamy, crowded and loud. It was perfect, with flags of the world draped from the ceilings and notes of all currencies tacked to the paint-peeling yellowed walls. A token effort had been made to string up a bit of tinsel, reminding us it was nearly Christmas – something we'd blissfully forgotten in our escape from the tedious festive wind-up. Soon we were pink-cheeked and leery, boisterously hugging for selfies, recounting our adventures as if we'd been at sea together for a lifetime. The crew, cut loose from the shackles of responsibility, looked relaxed, intent on a long night.

By midnight, my vision was beginning to blur a little. Kate was done too, and we headed back to the quiet of the ship, our ears ringing with residual cheer. *Europa*'s wooden decks gleamed in the smir as we stepped aboard for one last night on our ship. Across the bay, the lights of the town bled into the harbour as we stood at the stern rails, the spot where we'd spent so many hours taking in the extraordinary sights.

'I shall miss this,' said Kate. 'Back to travelling alone again.'

~

Your cramped room in the barracks houses four bunk beds, a small square table and two wooden chairs. It's damp, and the thin walls and windows rattle in the freshening gale. The window ledges fill up with snow.

'Don't leave any food out,' Eck tells you as you unpack your bag and settle in. 'Bloody rats. They overrun the place once the whaling ends and they've no more food.'

Late that night as you sleep, wrapped in thin grey blankets, the loud boom of an avalanche rolls down from the mountain peaks, startling you awake. The original whaling station here was once engulfed by an avalanche and was rebuilt further along the shore out of their path. You roll over and try to get back to sleep, but your heart races. You toss and turn for the rest of the night, waking from a brief doze in the morning, exhausted.

The toilets and showers are across the muddy lane down on the shore. As you poke your head around the door of the shower block, a large rat scuttles out of sight. The showers look unkempt and cold, so you don't bother to wash.

Most of the men spend all their time working, 8 a.m. to 8 p.m., squeezing in as much overtime as they can and double-pay on Sundays. It's work and bed, work and bed, day in, day out. You're assigned to the catchers, scraping the rust from their hulls and then painting, working well into the cold evenings, so chilled your breath hangs in the bright artificial lights.

At the end of each day, many of the men spend their time swapping the season's best yarns over illicit drinks in the cabins, the catches engorged with telling, the whales grown so large it's a wonder they were squeezed up the factory slip-way at all. Alcohol is banned by the whaling companies, but most of the whalers can make a passable brew using raisins, rice or oatmeal soaked in big Kilner jars. They beg yeast from the baker, mix it with water and sugar and call it 'soup' before distilling it in Baby Burco boilers. Black liquor is made from tins of boot polish heated over a stove and strained through a loaf of bread, and though the boots of the whale men are rarely cleaned, vast quantities of boot polish are sold in the slop-chest, along with aftershave and compass fluid – also used to augment their home brews. Some of it is lethal, and you keep well clear of it. If they're caught, they're put on a shilling a month and sent home on the first transport, though that would be a blessing for you. You don't join in with the men's evening sessions, determined not to go back to drinking again.

It's a miserable few weeks. But the *Opal* is due in soon. Maybe she'll bring news from home. The men who signed up to overwinter are beginning to regret their decision. The prospect of no news or contact from home for seven months is beginning to bite hard. The squalid barracks barely hold any heat, and the smell of the tiny four-berth cabins is worse than anything on the catchers. Rats are everywhere. Huge brown rats. And now it's so much colder they move into the barracks too, chewing through everything.

By early April the winter dark sets in, the days shorten. Though there is still some daylight, the steep peaks around the station mean the sun won't fall on it for six months. The whole place is dank and damp, and your clothes smell fusty. The winds, fierce and wild, wail down from the peaks, right through the flimsy buildings, sometimes tearing off the corrugated-iron roof sheets, flinging them down alongside the other morass of discarded debris lying around the station. When the snow falls, there is the daily drudge of shovelling. Sometimes the drifts tower high above your heads.

You wake one morning to see the catcher boats in the bay listing and in danger of capsizing with the weight of snowfall. You and the other men spend all day in the freezing sleet, clearing them off.

Still fitful in your bunk at night, it takes a huge effort for you to rise each morning. You're exhausted, your limbs aching and heavy from the constant grind. The shore boss calls you in to the office after your shift one evening.

'Tony, lad, you need to buck yourself up,' he tells you. 'The other men are complaining that you're not pulling your weight. They say you're slow and keep making mistakes. Is there anything wrong?'

You shake your head, confused. You thought you'd been doing okay, getting on with the job. He looks you up and down. 'You need to clean yourself up too, Tony. You're stinking. Get a shower and a change of clothes.'

You skip supper, your appetite gone. Back in the cabin, Eck is entertaining a couple of other lads with his stories of the *Soldier*'s season. A flagon of home-brew sits on the table, and the boys are leery and pink-cheeked. You refuse their offers of drink and take to your bunk with a book.

'He's not even reading it,' you hear one of the lads quietly joke, nodding over in your direction. 'He's not turned that page in half an hour now.'

Two days before the *Southern Opal* is due to arrive, Eck's having a get-together for his birthday. He invites you along to one of the other cabins for drinks. When you get there, it's loud and smoky. Eck welcomes you, shifting along in the bunk he's sitting on, making space for you and offering you a drink. But in the face of his kindness you find yourself in tears, mumbling about how no one likes you, how worthless you are. You don't even know where this is coming from.

'It's just the whale sickness,' one of the old hands tells you, patting you kindly on the shoulder. 'You're not the first, nor the last, to go down with it. You're just missing killing the whales now you've had a taste of it.'

But you've seen enough killing for a lifetime.

You leave, not wanting to spoil their fun, and return to your cabin, crawl into your bunk and pull the covers over your head.

~

Breakfast was a ragged affair after our night of high spirits in the bar, but the sun evaporated our groggy heads with the morning dew and we supped extra coffee out on deck before gathering the last of our things, stripping bedding from our bunks and rattling through the empty drawers and lockers to check for lost socks. The cabin, stark and bare, echoed, no longer the home we'd made for ourselves for the last six weeks. I wondered who might sleep in my bunk next.

At eleven, we gathered for our final farewell meeting in the deckhouse. Jordi showed us the book he'd put together of our voyage, detailing every place we'd visited, every change in the weather, every day of the entire six-week trip journalled alongside his spectacular photographs. The whole crew had worked tirelessly behind the scenes, while we'd only masqueraded as sailors. They looked exhausted, every last one of them, but also relieved at having delivered yet another contingent safely to shore. Their rest would be short, their season relentless, another group of eager guests arriving in just two days' time, and all the cleaning and reprovisioning to be done before then.

Before we left, the crew had organised an auction in aid of the South Georgia Heritage Trust: charts and maps, books, T-shirts, a digital set of Jordi's photographs, cuddly penguins and mugs. I half-heartedly bid on a few items without success. Then they held up a print of Elephant Island, looking from the sea towards Point Wild set against the stark mountains and fading light, shaded in muted purples and slate greys. The sea mirrored the moody sky stacked steep with clouds, the only brightness a ray of pale yellow sunlight spilling through a single rent in the dark skies. The print was titled *Cape Bloody Wild*, and I found myself bidding. One of the other passengers, a huge Shackleton fan, wanted it too, and the bids rose steeply, but I found my hand rising again and again until he gave up. Frank Wild's story had stuck with me. His relentless optimism in the face of the daily desperation, stranded so isolated on that tiny beach, resonated deeply with me. I had to buy this painting for G. In that brooding, bruised gloom, I recognised his daily struggle, the chronic depression he'd lived with for so long. I recognised how each and every morning he got up, looking in hope for that speck on the horizon, for a sign that this was the day he'd be rescued.

~

Finally, the *Southern Opal* comes in to port. You're woken in your cabin by the sound of her horn as she docks at the pier.

'That's put a smile on your face,' Eck says as you peer out the frosty window at the ship.

The *Opal* is loaded quickly, taking on mostly men and oil for the journey. There is no mail, but at least you're finally heading home.

Eager to board and claim your bunk, you stash your belongings in the cabin assigned to you. The *Opal* is a transport ship and more spacious than the *Venturer*, so there's plenty of room for everyone. You're looking forward to the warmth of sailing back through the tropics. It will be May when you arrive home in Scotland – the best time of year – the days lengthening into the full breadth of summer. Even the thought of it warms your bones.

That night before you leave, a party is held in one of the barracks' cabins and Eck invites you along to say goodbye to the men staying behind. This time, you're cheery and take a drink of the home-brew when offered. It reddens your cheeks and brings a warm glow to your belly. The men cheer you on, kind and back-slapping – glad to see you out of your slump. They have been busy, brewing, distilling, making black liquor from boot polish. The drinks keep flowing, and the room begins to swim a little, but you stay, feeling happier than you've felt for weeks.

~

I woke early, sprawled starfish-like in the huge bed of my hotel room, alone for the first time in six weeks. I'd slept fitfully, missing the rise and fall of the ocean to lull my sleep. Cars had raced up and down the street, horns blaring, for most of the night. The room felt huge, and every time I went into the bathroom, the walls swam and shifted around me as I grappled for my land-legs. I should have felt glad of my own space at last, and yet I missed my tiny cabin and the dance Kate and I had learned to do around each other in the cramped space.

Those of us who had stayed overnight in Ushuaia had met up the previous evening in a restaurant with a large central fire-pit and a spread-eagled sheep roasting over the flames. We were all neat and clean, our windswept hair tamed. Waiters piled huge platters of meat onto the table, and a big dish of roasted vegetables for me. We ate and drank with gusto but barely made a dent in so much food. I began to realise why the town's stray dogs looked so well fed. It had been a good evening, a last farewell before we scattered like a shoal of startled fish. Though it was sad to leave these friends behind, I knew we'd all stay in touch and meet again when we could, bound by the bonds of our extraordinary journey.

I packed up the last of my things and bumped along the potholed road in a taxi to Ushuaia airport. The small building on the outskirts of town stood next to the runway, right at the edge of the sea. A few of my shipmates from the *Europa* were there already, waiting for the same flight. They were not from my watch, and I hadn't got to know them well, but we sat and shared our stories as we waited for our flight to Buenos Aires. As we took off, I glanced back. Ushuaia looked beautiful: snow-capped mountains, glittered seas and that gorgeous high-latitude morning light, so like home, so like Scotland.

~

You stir. A vague recollection of a ship's horn. Then nothing. When you finally wake, you find yourself back on the *Southern Soldier*, not even in your own bunk. You don't remember how you got here. The boat is empty, now fully stripped out and laid up for the winter, not even blankets in the bunk. You are freezing, your head splitting, your mouth desert-dry – still with the foul taste of boot-polish liquor.

A panic surges as you begin to remember, to gather your thoughts. The slow realisation dawns that you are not where you are meant to be. You fumble your way out onto the deck and stand shivering in your shirt-sleeves in the cold sleet-grey day. You look out across the harbour, your eyes darting around the bay, searching all the way to the narrow strip of horizon. The pier is empty. The *Southern Opal* has sailed.

Part Three

NORTH

When a person is lost overboard and disappears into the sea, and if you are the one to see them fall, you must keep them in your sights as you raise the alarm. Do not look away, even for an instant, but keep looking at them, point towards them, arm outstretched as they recede into the distance. A bobbing head is easily lost, disappearing into the troughs of waves and swell. Glimpses might be snatched here and there, and then nothing. It's all too easy to lose sight – the ocean so vast, a person so small. But someone still ought to point. And if you do lose sight, there are search patterns to follow, protocols to be observed, structured ways of looking. But sometimes, it's all a bit of a shot in the dark.

7

Search Patterns

Though it's more than a year since I returned from Antarctica, I still feel the weight of Anthony Ford; the memory of his grave in South Georgia keeps surfacing. If I were not a scientist and a believer mostly in things that can be explained, I might say his soul is unsettled. I begin to tinker at the edges of a search.

Unsure of what I'm looking for, I start with what I know: his name. I find the record of his birth and, through it, trace his family history; perhaps there is a thread I can pick up. I find records of the places he lived, and his parents, grandparents and siblings. But none are alive now. It seems it is easy to go back in time through family trees, but to move forward, to find the living, is trickier.

In Edinburgh one day, I happen upon Drummond Street, and it takes me a while to remember how I know the name of this place: Anthony was born here. I find his building. It's tatty, so many of the windows boarded up. A quick dig on the Internet tells me David Bowie also once lived here. Anthony's birthplace was Ziggy Stardust's too.

And then I am at the McManus in Dundee, to see Frances Walker's Antarctic paintings. As I browse the museum downstairs, I find cabinets filled with bottles of whale oil, slices of baleen and finely etched scrimshaw – portraits and penguins carved onto sperm whales' teeth, curved and pointed like the tips of elephant tusks. Harpoons splay in an array of compass directions, progressing from hand-forged iron – one still bent and twisted from the fight of the last whale it speared – to the more modern gun-fired grenade-tipped steel harpoons. Photographs show stocky men dressed in the typical whalers' uniform of the nineteenth century – tweed trousers and gilets, long leather boots, white sailcloth smocks and fur hats.

Strung above my head are the bleached bones of a humpback. Under the flat plate of the skull, the lower jawbones embrace a Zodiac-sized pocket of museum air. The ribs hang below the spine like a driftwood cage, unconnected by a sternum. I imagine the breadth of its lungs, the size of its scarlet heart.

Dundee sent the first whale ships to the Arctic in the 1750s, and for 160 years, whaling provided employment, not just for seamen but also for shipwrights, blacksmiths, ropemakers, sail-makers, carters and merchants. Even when whale oil was replaced by coal gas in the 1820s and paraffin in the 1860s, local demand in Dundee remained high in the jute factories, where it was used to soften the fibres.

Arctic whaling came to an end before the First World War, whale stocks plundered to the thin end of extinction. Sights turned south. The Salvesen family moved into the industry, and the Edinburgh port of Leith became the Scottish hub of Antarctic whaling.

Months later, I stand at the carved oak doors of Trinity House in Leith, a museum cared for by Historic Scotland and open by appointment only. I've been told, though I can't remember by whom, that they have whaling diaries from a crew member on one of the factory ships. The guide opens the doors at the appointed time and invites me in; I am the only visitor that day. The marble entrance-hall floor is inset with the Trinity House coat of arms: an anchor, two globes and a compass, its ribboned motto wound around the edges. *Pervia virtuti Sydera, Terra, Mare* – the Earth, the sea and the stars are conquerable by men of courage – not an exact translation, but the one that has been chosen, the *conquerable by men* slipped in for good measure.

Before it was a museum, Trinity House, set up in 1380, cared for destitute sailors and their families. To fund itself, the foundation raised a levy on goods loaded and unloaded at Edinburgh's Leith Docks and later, in the eighteenth century, trained licensed pilots to guide ships in and out of the Forth. Today, the stately sandstone building, completed in 1818, stands on the vaults of the original alms houses, tucked away in the back lanes of Leith. There is not even the noise of traffic to mask the fall of our footsteps as the guide shows me around the rooms and allows me ample time and space to view the collection of priceless paintings, antiques and maritime curios packed into its oak-panelled interiors. Up the imperial staircase, in the splendid Convening Room, a long dining table serves up a buffet of maritime artefacts: sextants, gimballed compasses, ships' bells, pocket watches, star globes, sail-makers' tools, narwhal tusks and harpoons. The afternoon sun slants through the windows, glinting on the steady fall of motes we've stirred up; I pity those tasked with the dusting.

From the faded crimson walls, men in Georgian attire stare down at us: a whale-ship owner and a Royal Navy admiral immortalised by Edinburgh artist Henry Raeburn.

At the far end of the room hangs a huge painting of Portuguese explorer Vasco da Gama navigating a ship through a storm, smoke-dark from years of hanging above a fireplace, only the feart sailors' faces peeking from the gloom.

A rounded chunk of bone sits on a mantelpiece. The guide nods his permission for me to pick it up.

'Do you know what it is?' he asks. I shake my head. 'A whale's eardrum.'

It feels smooth and tactile, about the size and shape of a Cornish pasty. There are several in the museum's collection, some carved into scrimshaw and one painted as a grotesque court jester.

I ask about the whalers' diaries, but the guide knows nothing about them and advises me to contact Historic Scotland. If they do exist, they sit in an archive somewhere. As interesting as I find the museum, there is no trace of Anthony and his like in these time-capsuled rooms, gunnel-full of treasure long ago traded for the lives of whales.

I begin to edge a little closer, though. I discover Edinburgh University library has a long shelf of records in its basement recovered from the Salvesen office in Bernard Street when it closed in 1999. Not everything, I'm told, just a sample, and the library sends me a thirty-two page document listing every item: vessel reports, whaling logs, lists of infractions, bills of sale, notes from management dinner discussions, lists of films to be shown at Leith Harbour, lists of ships, letters, plans, photographs and crew records. I email Rachel Hosker, the archivist in charge. Might they have any records of an Anthony Ford? She replies to tell me he was on the crew list for the *Southern Venturer* for the seasons 1949–50 and 1951–52. The document is restricted, though, and not available for viewing. Is there anything else I'd like to see?

Box B2 contains letters from a crew member of the *Southern Venturer* to his family. Someone from the same ship, dated for the same journey Anthony sailed on to South Georgia in 1949, aged sixteen. There is no name, and I daren't hope they are from him. But still, someone on the same voyage. 'May I see them?' I ask. And also the ship's log book and catch reports for the *Southern Venturer* for the 1951–52 season, his last, and the consignment book detailing the commodities brought back to Liverpool Docks that year. These other things are unlikely to tell me anything about him, but I want some small glimpse into the day-to-day of his life. I set a date to visit.

On the top floor of the library at Edinburgh University, a light glass-walled space houses the collections office, where people pore over rare books, drawings, photographs, plans and artwork. On the tables, bean-filled cushions support leather-bound tomes in just the right way so as not to break their spines. People wear gloves and take notes as sunlight floods into the temperature-controlled rooms. This refuge gives sanctuary to the past.

When I arrive, Rachel takes me in to a small side room filled with low chairs and colourful artworks. 'Sorry about this, but we have to take the privacy of these records very seriously. Some of the people are still alive. You're not allowed to mention anyone by name. The letters are really interesting – I think you'll get a lot out of them. But you mustn't write anything that might identify the person that wrote them. Not his name or position. Is that okay?'

We pass through a locked glass door into the collections viewing room. The documents are laid out on a trolley behind the desk. I must ask for each in turn and return it before I'm allowed to look at the next. I begin with the letters and move to a table close to the window. The view opens out across Edinburgh's rooftops. It's a clear September day, and a few cirrus clouds whisk across the cityscape. I open the folder. The walls of the library fade, and I am all at sea again.

The letters are not from Anthony. But there are pages of tightly crammed words on oh-so-delicately-thin sheets of A5 paper. For an entire afternoon, I travel with the writer on his journey south.

Let's call him Thomas. He is on his first voyage, his first job after years of studying, and he writes to share every moment with his family. I imagine them in their airy drawing room gathered to hear his letters read aloud. *Mary, fetch the children. We have a letter from Thomas*, they would tell their maid.

Thomas has a cabin to himself on the *Southern Venturer*, a sink with running water, a table, couch, chair and reading lamps. *It's very comfortable*, he writes. He is young and excited for his first voyage. The ship stops to refuel in Tenerife, where stowaways sneak aboard. They are caught in a terrifying storm in the Roaring Forties. On reaching South Georgia, the ship pays a brief visit to Leith Harbour to drop off the catcher crews before she heads south.

At first, Thomas writes of the sun barely dipping below the horizon at night, bathing the ice in sunset colours. He writes of the glittering icebergs and wild seas. But then he writes of the relentless graft. The work is interesting, and Thomas enjoys it initially, but as his letters become shorter, more perfunctory, the excitement is gone and replaced with resignation. His boss becomes depressed and locks himself in his cabin and refuses to come out. Thomas is left to pick up the work of two men, seven days a week.

As the *Southern Venturer* ends her season and heads back towards South Georgia, the weather turns cold and wild. Thomas braces himself against a bulkhead to write his final letter home: *I shall never regret this trip. It has been a hard life indeed, tougher than anything I have ever done before. The strain on the nerves has been great. I have done 13½ weeks without a break.*

It's the last letter in the pile. The walls of the library come back into focus, and I soften my gaze to the Edinburgh skyline. As I carefully restack the sheaves of paper and put them back into the folder, a small unmarked envelope falls to the desk. I put on pale blue nitrile gloves and pull out six black-and-white photographs. They've been taken on board the ship. Nothing is written on the backs. The first photo: ten blue whales towed, belly up, from the stern of the ship, flocks of cape petrels swarming the seas around them. The second photo: a female fin whale, giant mouth gaping at the sea, dragged by her tail up the ship's stern slipway. The third shows the lemmers thigh-deep in chunks of meat, the carcass of a whale stripped ready for the bonesawmen. In the fourth photo, men heave a huge chunk of meat across the deck towards the boiler hatch. In the fifth, a man stands next to a pile of pale intestines slithering on the deck, ready for shoving overboard. And then the last photograph: a blue whale mother lies on the deck, her belly split throat to tail. Her baby – a foetus – maybe six feet long, has been pulled from her. An older man leers at the camera as his hands haul open the baby's mouth for the photographer. And there, in the background. A tall lad, flat-capped and jacketed, his mouth agape, stares at the dead baby. Written stark across his face: the horror.

And I think, *It's him. It's Anthony.*

*

Rain blatters windows already blotched with October leaves. I warm my hands on a mug of tea to watch *Britain's Whale Hunters*, a documentary from 2014 filmed on South Georgia, presented by Adam Nicolson. In it, Nicolson wanders around Leith Harbour whaling station. He has access to those places out of bounds to us through dilapidation and asbestos. He wears a blue paper boiler suit and face-mask, the kind worn by forensic teams. If the whaling station seemed eerie from the outside, it is even more so inside. The weather is good, the sky bright as he clambers over rusted corrugated-iron sheets and wanders down Pig Street, now grassed over.

'It's like it's been burgled,' Nicolson says, walking into one of the offices, pulling out drawers of records and index cards. Anthony's name must be in there somewhere.

Nicolson pokes around the living quarters where pin-up-girl pictures are still tacked to the walls. Then he visits the hospital. In a small whitewashed room, empty except for a cast-iron bed frame, Nicolson holds up a computer tablet to show a photograph of a man in the same room, ashen as he sits in the bedside chair. The pharmacy on the second floor is still stacked with medicines. He picks a few up – kaolin, adrenaline, dried blood plasma. Coloured pills are scattered across shelves and on the floor.

Nicolson wanders into the manager's office. 'Nicest room in the whole place,' he remarks, taking in the grand desks. Leather-bound books sit on the shelves, and a large window overlooks the bay. He sits down in one of the chairs and talks about Salvesen's annual profits – over £1 million – £73 million in today's money. This was a mega-industry of its day.

I've been reading about the Salvesen family. They ran a tight business with few shareholders and kept profits largely within the family. Today, many Salvesen descendants are wealthy off the back of the family fortunes. Alastair Salvesen, great-grandson of founder Christian Salvesen, is one of Scotland's few billionaires and lives on a large estate in Midlothian. His brother Robin owns an estate in nearby East Lothian. I wonder about the paintings they have on their walls, the artefacts lying on their shelves, like those at Trinity House.

Meanwhile, responsibility for the tangled mess, contamination and pollution left behind on South Georgia reverted to the British Government – to the British taxpayer. The South Georgia Heritage Trust, a charity, took on the task of raising donations to deal with the scourge of rats let loose by the ships and now decimating the indigenous populations of ground-nesting birds. The rats thrived on an abundance of eggs and young chicks, and the unique South Georgia pipit was reduced to surviving in just a few tiny pockets of the island between glacier snouts, where the rats could not reach. With the warming climate, the glaciers were beginning their swift retreat from the shore, now allowing the rats a free run of the entire island.

It's a story as old as capitalism. Company owners and shareholders accruing wealth at the expense of the environment and the taxpaying public: the oil companies still unearthing fossil fuels and walking away from the climate crisis; the agro-industries deforesting the Amazon and Indo-Pacific nations for beef grazing and palm oil; the industrial-scale trawlers scraping the life out of our oceans.

Whale stocks exhausted, Salvesen left the whaling industry in 1963 after it ceased to become profitable. It invested in its logistics expertise, running a major European transport business. The Christian Salvesen Company was eventually sold in 2007 for £254.4 million.

Nicolson moves on to the old kino – the cinema at the Leith Harbour whaling station – and talks about how the profits were ploughed back into making life better for the whalers. But the men's old payslips show the cinema subscription docked from their wages – they paid for it themselves. Iain Dick, whose father was a whaler, remembers going along to the Salvesen Office in Bernard Street with his mother to collect her fortnightly allotment. He recalls 'old Salvesen' giving him a huge £5 note at Christmas. Iain felt overawed by the generosity of the man. Only years later did he learn that Salvesen deducted the money from his father's wage at the end of the season.

The men earned good money, though, depending on bonuses and the length of their time away. In Nicolson's documentary, men from the Salvesen Ex-Whalers Club are interviewed, now in their late seventies and eighties. One talks of being paid off at the end of an eighteen-month stretch with £1,100 – at a time when the average house cost £600.

Nicolson explores the outside of the whaling station and climbs into one of the giant tanks, crumpled under the force of the wind, and wonders aloud how many dead whales it would have taken to fill it with oil. He makes his way to the old ski jump on the southern edge of the station. He tells how the men competed in their own makeshift winter games, and footage shows them careering down the same ski jump. The music is upbeat in that jolly 1950s wasn't-it-all-such-fun kind of way. But then, the mood changes, a more sombre tone adopted. 'Life on a remote Antarctic island wasn't for every-one,' Nicolson says.

The footage cuts to an interview with Tommy Yorkston, a compact man wearing a smart blue blazer.

'It's a long time, eighteen months, a long time to be away from home,' he says. 'Sometimes you got a wee bit fed up, wanting to be back home again.'

Depression among the men, especially over winter, was so rife they had a special name for it. Even the doctors fell to using the term.

The film cuts back to Nicolson walking away from the station, the hood on his paper boiler suit now down. 'Dr MacIntosh talks about whale sickness that seems to have afflicted a lot of people,' he says.

Nan Brown spent three years on South Georgia as the wife of a radio-station operator. She describes whale sickness in her book *Antarctic Housewife* as 'truculent behaviour, moping and imaginary complaints being typical symptoms for which there is only one cure – a good catch of whales'.

To this day, depression is poorly understood, and though we talk more openly about it, people often still use pejorative terms. As recently as 2007, scientists from King's College London asked a cohort of fourteen-year-old students what words they might use to describe someone with mental-health issues. More than half of the 250 words they came up with were derogatory. Among the kinder terms listed were *disturbed, attention seekers, feeling sorry for themselves, strange, stressed, touchy, troubled, weirdo, moody, unhappy, vulnerable, unstable.*

As in Nan Brown's description, there is often a strong implied element of blame on the sufferer, seen as deserving of little sympathy. Among a culture of such denial, which was of its time, it is likely that whalers suffering depression were at best shunned, or at worst ridiculed and ostracised.

Nicolson continues his tour. 'But for some people, depression could be a lot worse than that,' he says, walking away from the camera and over a bridge towards the graveyard, the same one I stood in two years before. He walks up and down the lines of graves. 'They are all so young,' he says. 'Twenty-five, thirty-seven, twenty-nine.'

The film cuts back to Tommy. His eyes drift up to the right. His face falls. 'There's a friend of mines down there . . . he just lost the plot. A boy called Tony Ford. He come from Edinburgh.'

As I hear this, my hand jabs at the pause button to stop the film; I don't want to hear what comes next. I take a moment before I'm ready to hit play again.

Nicolson walks on to stand at the foot of his grave. 'Here's Tony Ford.' He brings out his tablet. 'I've got a record here of his death. Cause of death: strangulation. Coroner's inquest: suicide while balance of mind disturbed.' Nicolson's head drops, visibly upset.

And there he is.

'A pitiable end. Poor man. Poor boy,' ends Nicolson, as he walks away from the graveside.

I wrap up in my warmest jacket and scarf, throw a waterproof over the top and hike up to the ridge above our house, barely stopping to catch my breath, needing to be in the midst of the gale. This wasn't the story I'd thought for Anthony. When I found his grave, I'd imagined for him a heroic death. Because this is what we expect from the Antarctic, isn't it? Dying in pursuit of adventure. Immortalised in ice. Death from chasing glory. As I crest the ridge, the wind wraps around me like a stole, and I stop and let it take my weight. The rain stings my face, diluting my tears. I'm upset for Anthony, but it's also scratched a raw nerve: the memory of my friend Jamie.

I'd met Jamie in Spain, just after finishing university; he was between jobs. Both of us purposeless, we'd found ourselves living back in our family homes, so we hung out all summer. Jamie spoke fluent Spanish and knew all the best bars.

My parents were in the midst of a divorce, and I'd discovered a whole lot of unsavoury things about my dad, whom, to that point, I'd had firmly on a pedestal. I had no job and no money, and had not lived with my mother since I was fifteen; we'd butted too hard against each other back then. But by the time she left my dad, this fierce woman had turned into a meek shell of herself, and I missed her.

Jamie and I had vastly different lives. His family had wealth; he was stylish, sociable, had gorgeous girlfriends and liked to party all night and sleep all day. I was more of a loner and spent my days in the mountains, dressed in baggy dungarees and espadrilles, imagining I was Laurie Lee or some such character, walking among the heat-hazed, herb-scented limestone landscape as the distant toll of a church bell echoed across the valley. I'm not sure how we became such good friends. But Jamie was always kind. He had a quiet depth to him and took me under his wing. We'd go clubbing, dance and drink way too much, and then on our way home in the early hours of the morning, we'd stop in the orange groves and pick ice-cold fruit – tart and clean to our smoke-corrupted taste buds – and talk until the crimson dawn yawned from the sea. Jamie brought me out of my slump, gave me back my fighting spirit and that, in turn, gave my mum back hers.

At the end of the summer, I went back to university – I'd been offered a PhD at Stirling. He went back to his party life in London. We kept in touch now and again, but our lives were so different.

Two years later, Jamie was back in Spain, at rock bottom with depression and addiction after a series of failed jobs and unhealthy relationships. I wrote a few times but never heard back. Six months later, he took his own life – in the same way as Anthony.

Dr Jennifer Keys spent a year on South Georgia in 2005 as a medical officer. During her time there, and with access to the archive data, she took an interest in the medical history of the island and wrote about it for her Masters dissertation in 2008. I find a copy online. It's a catalogue of misery, not only for the litany of regular accidents described by the various South Georgia doctors over the years, but also because of the conditions in which the men worked. The whaling companies found it difficult to recruit doctors, and many were either very newly qualified or were persons with 'a history'.

Jennifer Keys's research found mental illness and suicide as common occurrences. Without naming him directly, she mentions Anthony's case and talks about him having missed his boat home. At the age of eighteen, he'd been a whaler for four years, she says.

One of the doctors on the factory ship, Robert Robertson, had answered an advert in the *British Medical Journal* in 1950, placed by Salvesen, for an experienced physician. Though Robertson practised as a psychiatrist, he was also an eccentric and adventurer, and he signed up for a season so he could study the 'modern whaleman' in his own habitat. Robertson and Anthony likely sailed on the same ship that year.

Through the post, I receive a copy of Robertson's book *Of Whales and Men* (the precursor to his later volume, *Of Sheep and Men*). It's old library stock from Stratford College, Virginia, hardbound in blue card with thick, yellowing pages roughly cut at their edges.

Robertson was obsessed with whaling, the old-fashioned sort anyway, and read everything he could on the New Bedford and Nantucket whalers. 'Inevitably,' he wrote, 'I was Ishmael,' and he aimed to enlighten the world on the lives of this new breed of whale men. He doesn't mention depression or whale sickness, though at least one man took his own life on his watch, and in reality depression affected the whalers, the overwinterers in particular, in large numbers. A few of the doctors themselves succumbed to it, often using alcohol or drugs to self-medicate.

Two versions of Robertson's book were published: the first in the US in 1954 and a later one in the UK. The one I receive in the post is the US edition, the one I wanted. In it, Robertson gives a frank and uncensored account of the conditions he found at the Leith Harbour whaling station. He'd been taken on a tour intended to show off the production process, but Robertson was more interested in the facilities for the men. There were none – only a pitiable library and shoddily built cinema. Robertson was appalled by the stench and filth of the whaling station and the conditions the men had to endure. He met the German doctor Hillenbrand, who, in his unpublished memoirs, describes the Leith Harbour 'hospital hut' as having a perished canvas ceiling directly beneath a corrugated-iron roof, which cast a thick layer of dust onto the operating table. Hillenbrand told Robertson how Salvesen refused to evacuate badly injured men and made them wait out the season until the factory or supply ships returned home.

Keys reports that after the publication of Robertson's book in the US, Salvesen threatened to sue him over his criticism of the conditions. The book was harmful to their reputation, they said. Gerald Elliot later inferred in *A Whaling Enterprise* that much of what Robertson wrote was fiction, and said that many ex-whalers agreed. But Elliot was the great-grandson of Christian Salvesen, and had spent most of his career working for the company. Robertson rewrote the chapter on Leith Harbour for the UK edition. The chapter, originally titled 'South Atlantic Slum', was replaced with one called 'South Atlantic Sanctuary', which talked only about the wildlife. The Leith Harbour chapter was moved to the end as an addendum and was considerably watered down, omitting the damning accusations against the whaling company. 'Perhaps my standards are a little too high,' Robertson added.

I search for Salvesen Ex-Whalers Club and turn up the Citadel Arts Group in Leith. They have just released a booklet, *Whaling Days*, to record the memories of the Leith whalers. Co-founder Liz Hare sends me a copy, filled with photographs, stories and anecdotes from the men, and I recognise a few from Nicolson's documentary. Liz also sends me details for the Whalers Club, and I make contact, asking after Anthony's friend Tommy from the documentary, though I'm unsure how to explain my interest in a long-dead young lad who lived well over sixty years ago, one that I've no family connection to.

Jimmy Yorkston, Tommy's brother, replies to my email: they are having a lunch for the club in February, and I'm invited. Tommy will be there and can perhaps tell me more about Anthony.

As the meeting draws closer, I feel anxious. I don't know what questions to ask, and I'm worried about the food. An invitation out to eat is always a challenge for vegans, and I don't want it to be *a thing*. I don't want these men to feel judged – that's not what I'm there for. I phone the hotel in advance and ask. They have something suitable on the menu.

The Rockville Hotel is an old-fashioned cube of a building abutting the Portobello shore. I'm early, so I park along the seafront and walk a while. Railings run the length of the promenade, and ornate cast-iron Victorian shelters face out to sea. The estuary is flat calm, a gull-speckled sea-glass green. Across the water, I can see the sketchy outline of Fife and to the east, the faint lump of Berwick Law.

As I walk back towards the hotel, I see a steady stream of men arrive, some in groups, some on their own. Many are stooped and use walking sticks. Nearly all are white-haired, wearing blazers and metal pin badges on their lapels. They could be mistaken for British Legion members, a group of ex-soldiers. They slowly gather as I ready myself to go in.

8

The Last Whalers

In the front bar, I recognise Jimmy from the documentary. I introduce myself, and he wraps my hand in both of his. My nerves settle with the simplicity of this warm gesture. Jimmy has a beautiful broad smile framed by a trimmed white beard. He too wears a smart blazer and enamel badges on his lapel.

Jimmy had followed his older brother Tommy into the whaling and worked four seasons in the late fifties and early sixties as a mess boy on the *Southern Harvester*.

'So tell me about your visit to South Georgia,' he asks, and we chat about my trip. He gets me a drink at the bar and waves away my offers to pay.

'It's all on the club today,' he says.

Just before we go through to the dining room, he lowers his voice and cautions me: Don Lennie, their treasurer, passed away two weeks ago. I feel awkward intruding on their grief.

Jimmy takes me through to the back room of the hotel. The decor is chintzy, floral curtains, thick carpets and tables laid out with sauce sachets in plastic baskets. Panoramic windows open straight out to the full width of the Forth estuary with no beach or foreshore between hotel and sea. It feels like we're on a ship. I see why they meet here, these men with the oceans still in their bones.

The dark wooden tables are set up in a T-shape, and the committee sits at the top table, their backs to the sea. Jimmy takes me to meet the chairman, George Cummings. He's thin and wiry with a wispy short beard. George is on edge. 'Yes, yes,' he says as Jimmy introduces me, 'but we have important things to discuss today. We need to make a decision about the club, so I don't want anything to get in the way of that.'

George, I find out, is an artist, and his exquisitely detailed paintings of the whaling factory ships and catcher boats, set against the backdrop of ice-strewn seas and the peaks of South Georgia, are displayed around the world, including two in the Sandefjord whaling museum in Norway. George read the stories of Scott and Shackleton as a boy and found himself drawn to Antarctica. He discovered Salvesen sailed there, and at the age of fifteen, without telling his parents, he took himself down to Bernard Street and signed up. When he was paid off at the end of his first season, he went home to his mother and threw a wad of money into the air.

George tells me later that he went back to South Georgia in 1991 on a cruise ship. While most of the tourists had gone off to Stromness, the crew put him ashore at Leith Harbour and let him walk alone up to the graveyard. He laid flowers for the station manager who'd been killed falling between two catchers when George had worked there. He took photos of the flowers on the grave and sent them to the man's wife in Norway. He laid flowers for Anthony too.

I take a seat near the bottom of the T and introduce myself to the men on either side of me. I ask how often they meet.

'Three to four times a year,' John MacLean says. 'The club is marvellous: they organise outings, we've been to whisky distilleries, boat trips, museums. And most years there's a trip to Norway too, where we meet the Norwegian whalers.'

Their camaraderie has endured well over sixty years. Whatever bonds were forged on those whaling ships had only strengthened.

John tells me how his uncle got him a job with Salvesen in 1960. He signed up, aged fifteen, as a mess boy for the winter at Leith Harbour and the following season on the *Southern Venturer*. He remembers coming ashore at South Georgia in the dark, and as he stood on the dock in the duffel coat bought by his mum, the realisation hit him that it would be more than a year before he'd get home again. 'The homesickness began that night,' he says. 'It was a real physical pain and didn't go away for a full two months.' John had his sixteenth and seventeenth birthday on South Georgia before he finally made it back home.

The room burbles with chat as waitresses bring out pints of beer for the men and coax out their orders between conversations.

At the end of the top table I recognise Tommy and slip out of my seat, crouching down at his side to say hello. We barely exchange pleasantries before he launches into his story about Anthony – primed and anxious to get it off his chest. Even after sixty-seven years, this is difficult.

'We grew up together,' he tells me. 'Tony lived across the road from me in Granton. We went to school together. I was there when he died.' He rushes through the sorry saga. Tommy tells me they'd all been drinking the night before they were due to return home on the *Southern Opal*, at the end of the season.

'The next day, Anthony slept in and missed his boat home. All of his things were already on the *Opal*,' Tommy says. 'He begged one of the catcher captains to take him out to meet up with the ship, but they wouldn't.' Tommy pauses and takes a breath. 'He took a rope and strung it over a bar from the ceiling in his dormitory. That's where we found him.' He looks down at the floor.

'I'm so sorry,' I say.

Out on the estuary, at Tommy's back, a long red tanker, low in the water, catches my eye as it heads west, upriver towards Grangemouth. After a pause I ask why he went to South Georgia. I can't tread rough-shod on this grief any longer.

'The money,' Tommy replies, breaking into an impish smile, his composure regained. 'The first year I came back off the whaling, I bought my dad a car and my younger brother Jimmy a new motorbike. The money was that good. You'd nothing to spend it on when you were down there, of course.'

The food begins to arrive, so I thank Tommy and suggest we might chat more later.

A toast is raised to Don Lennie, and we tuck in to our meals. My pasta Neapolitan escapes notice.

I ask the men at my end of the table about the jobs they did on the whaling ships.

'Mess boys – we were all mess boys here,' John tells me, looking around him. 'All except Bill there.' He points to a gentleman further up the table. 'He ran the slop-chest at Leith Harbour. He's a hundred years old now.' I smile at Bill, who looks a fit seventy.

'Aye. Even got my telegram from the queen,' he says.

'They sold everything in the stores, you know,' John says. 'Fancy watches, cameras, music boxes and trinkets to take home for girlfriends.'

'Mind that Omega watch you sold me, Bill?' Tommy shouts down from the top table. 'I brought it back after two weeks because it stopped working.'

'Aye,' chuckles Bill. 'You didnae ken you had to wind it up!'

'I'd never had a watch before,' laughs Tommy. 'I've still got it. It's still working. As long as I remember to wind it, mind.'

After we've eaten, George chinks his glass with a knife. The hubbub dies down. He stands and begins with a tribute to Don Lennie. A few of the men dab at their eyes with white cotton handkerchiefs.

Don, an engineer, worked on oil tankers before he went whaling, a luxurious job compared to life on a catcher boat where he found himself after signing up with Salvesen. After his first season, he went back to work on a tanker, but the call of the whaling was too strong, and he transferred back at the start of the following season; little could compete with the adventure and comradeship of a catcher boat. Don was clearly a character who would be sorely missed at these meetings.

'So we've lost our treasurer, and sadly, our numbers are reducing every year,' George says. 'Having a formal club is a lot of work. We have to chase up subscriptions, keep financial records, type up minutes and send out newsletters.' He was beginning to get a little emotional, clearing his throat, shuffling his notes. 'I'd like to propose that today we formally end the club. We can meet more informally once a year instead, but it's just too much work to keep it all going.' The men around the room look tired. Even an outing for lunch is a stretch for some. They nod in agreement.

Jimmy raises his hand. 'I'll second that proposal, George.'

'Okay, thank you, Jimmy. Let's take a vote on it.' The rest of the men raise their hands in favour, nod and murmur their approval.

'Carried,' George says. Looking around at the men, the anxiety lifts from his face. It is the end of an era for these men, but the time had come.

They rise from their chairs and circulate, catching up with friends they've not yet had a chance to see. To my left, Jimmy and Tommy stand with a man I recognise as Danny Morrison from Nicolson's documentary. They huddle together, talking in low voices, but I overhear snatches of their conversation. They are talking about me.

'It seems a funny thing to be asking . . . after all these years.'

'What does she want to know? It's a bit strange.'

'. . . his death certificate, the cause . . . perhaps she thinks there's more to it.'

Shit, shit, shit. They think I'm on some cold-case hunt for a murderer. That's not why I'm here to meet them. I feel so awkward, mad at myself for being so intrusive. Heat rises up my neck. John, next to me, is talking, but I don't hear his words. In my head, I'm cursing myself, annoyed at my stupid obsession. I excuse myself and head to the bathroom.

The ladies' toilet has a tall narrow window that looks straight out to sea. It's open, and I draw in breaths of the cold breeze, the scent of seaweed and salt. I close my eyes and tune in to the sound of waves lapping at the shore. *Just trust that you're here for a reason*, I tell myself.

When I take my place back at the table, Danny sits down next to me and introduces himself. He wears a Norwegian-style jumper patterned across the shoulders; a short split at the front is fastened with two ornate pewter clasps. Slim, upright and agile, he looks fit for his age. He hands me a card filled with names and phone numbers.

'Go on, test me,' he says. 'Give me a name off the card and I'll tell you the number.' I pick a name, and he reels off the number perfectly; there are around fifty on the card. 'Have to keep the old brain active at my age,' he says, tapping the side of his head with his forefinger. 'What do you want to know?' he asks, looking at me directly. I steer clear of asking anything else about Anthony.

'I'd just like to hear more of your stories. I had so little idea about whaling before I went to South Georgia.' I ask how he came to be a whaler. I know this story – it's in Liz Hare's *Whaling Days* book – but I'm guessing it's the one he most loves to tell, and I'd like to hear him tell it.

He tips back his head and laughs, looking at me sideways. 'Well, that's a funny story,' he says launching into his tale. After Danny's father died during the war, his mother was left to bring up three children on her own, on 10 shillings a week. She shared out what little food they had equally and would always say a prayer before they ate. One evening, Danny watched as his mother put a plate of three fried eggs on the table for their tea. 'I asked if I could say grace,' Danny says. 'My mother was surprised, but she agreed. I closed my eyes, put my hands together and said, "Dear God, three eggs between four of us, thank God there's no more of us." My mother was furious. She picked up the plate and broke it square over my head. A few days later, I was marched down to the Salvesen office and signed up for South Georgia. It meant she could feed the other two and get an allotment from my wages as well.'

Danny was one of the longest-serving whalers, having worked seventeen seasons including five winters and even a double winter once. He grew up near Leith Docks, in a two-room flat shared between two families – ten of them in all, and no electricity. He started as a mess boy on the *Southern Harvester* in 1946 and went down to Middlesborough Docks, where she was still being built. The new ship was luxury for Danny – his own bunk and hot showers, something he'd never had before.

Danny found the factory work dull, but after a couple of years he landed a job as an able seaman on a catcher and went on to work his way up to second mate. He was a great skier too, training hard to beat the Norwegians at their own game. Danny was one of the few Brits who could land from the ski jump at Leith Harbour. He'd spend his winter evenings running circuits around the station to get fit for the annual skiing competition between the three South Georgia whaling stations.

Jimmy and Tommy join us at the table and begin with their anecdotes too, polished and honed like curling stones, slipping each other lines and reminders, sliding their tales back and forth between them, smoothing the pathways of memory.

'Mind that penguin you had at Leith Harbour, Tommy?' Danny says.

'Oh aye. Poor wee fella got covered in oil. I found him on the shore at Leith Harbour and cleaned him off with detergent, covered his wee eyes an' everything. After that, though, he wouldn't go back in the water and took to following me about. I used to catch rock cod from the shore for him with a bent nail on a string. There were that many fish you didn't even need bait back then. I had to leave him there at the end of the season, though.'

Tommy worked his way up to engineer on one of the catchers and finished whaling in 1958 when he got called up for National Service. His experience stood him in good stead, and he worked as an engineer on nuclear power plants all over the world.

'I started as a wee laddie in a council house in Granton, and now I've got a lovely big house in Dunbar,' he says, beaming.

'What about that time you got rammed by the sperm whale – remember that?' Jimmy prompts.

Tommy is on a roll now, relaxed and loosened up. 'Aye, that was on the *Southern Archer*. The gunner shot this sperm whale, but it went through the tail and out the other side. The whale turned right around and headed back towards us and rammed its head into our propeller. What a jolt we got! We thought we were going under, but she righted herself again. We had to go into Melbourne to get the boat fixed. That was a treat. It was in the local papers there an' all.'

A few of the men are beginning to disperse, and Jimmy and Danny get up to see them off and say their goodbyes.

'We even caught a two-headed whale once too,' Tommy continues.

'A two-headed whale?' My eyebrows arch.

'Aye, it was a baby, cut out of its mother. Came out with two heads and one tail. I've still got a photo of it. Never seen such a thing in all my life.'

Before I can ask more, Tommy gets called over to say goodbye to a few of the men. As they mingle and say their cheerios, a softly spoken man sitting opposite me introduces himself as Ian, but I don't quite catch his surname. He's been quiet for most of the meal, listening in to the chat. Unlike the others, he doesn't wear a blazer nor any badges; he's in a fleece jacket and collared shirt. His eyes are a rheumy blue. I ask him if he'd been a mess boy too.

'Aye, yes. I was a mess boy too, like the others.' Ian had always wanted to go whaling as a young lad. He came from a small village in the Highlands and had never even been to a city when he first sent a letter to Salvesen, at the age of twelve. 'I wrote to them every year, always on the lookout for new adventures,' he says. 'When I turned fifteen, they finally said they would take me if my father gave his permission, which he did. We went to the office in Leith and I got signed up there and then. I only did one season, though.'

'Why only one?'

Ian pauses, looking out the broad window and across the wide estuary; white-flecked waves beckon in the wind. 'I started on the factory ship, and that was fine, but I'd always wanted to go on one of the catchers. It was the thrill of the chase, you see. All the men loved it on the catchers. That's where the excitement happened.'

He told me how one day the chief steward had approached him to ask if he would swap with another lad struggling with seasickness. The catchers were so much smaller and prone to being bounced about on the rough seas.

'They were hit hard with every wave, and by God it could be rough on those seas.'

I knew what he meant, remembering our own wild journey down to South Georgia, and I'm sure we'd not even glimpsed the fury that ocean could unleash. Our ship was also sturdier than any catcher boat. Ian had jumped at the chance to swap and transferred the following day.

'It was great fun, every bit as exciting as I'd imagined.' Ian pauses and looks down at his feet. 'Except one day, we caught this big blue whale, but the harpoon didn't explode properly, and she wasn't killed outright. She fought for ages but eventually tired, and we hauled her alongside the boat. I was standing right beside her then. Just before the gunner fired another harpoon into her, she rolled over and looked straight at me, eye to eye, from just a few feet away. I must be one of the very few people in the world to have looked a blue whale in the eye like that. And in that moment, I just knew she was a living soul. And I knew she recognised me as one too.' The tears began to roll down his face. 'After that, I never wanted to go whaling again.' His head drops. Through the open window, I hear the quiet lap of waves on the shore. When he looks up he says, 'I'm sorry, you must think I'm such a softie. Daft crying over an animal like that after all this time.' He pulls out a handkerchief to wipe away his tears and collects himself.

'I don't think you're daft at all.' I fight back my own tears.

It is the final story I need for Anthony, the last piece in the puzzle to make sense of his life, of his death. I know now why I've come here to talk to these men. I needed to find some humanity in the wreckage and bones abandoned on that island.

As I leave, I say goodbye to Jimmy.

'Did you get what you came for?'

I nod and thank him.

'Most people don't want to hear our stories,' he says. 'When people find out I'm a whaler, they always ask me how I could have killed a whale. And I always tell them, I didn't kill whales. I made soup, I washed dishes. And that's the truth.'

A few days later, an A4 brown envelope drops through my letterbox. In it, a copy of a faded photograph: a long fin-whale foetus lies flaccid on a flensing plan, its papery thin flukes still softened by amniotic fluid, the dorsal fin flopped to the side. It's fully formed, not long before birth, blowhole, rostrum and eyes clearly visible, the underside of the pale lower jaw fluted and grooved. But from its left side protrudes a second complete head, blowhole at the top, lying alongside the first; it really is a two-headed whale. Behind it, kneeling on the deck, a young man in a collared jacket and flat cap looks towards the tail. If he'd lain down beside it, the whale would be a few feet longer than he is tall.

It seems a two-headed whale is exceedingly rare but not unheard of. In 2017, Dutch fishermen caught a two-headed porpoise while trawling in the North Sea. Its two heads shared a tail, just like the whale in Tommy's photo. The fishermen had photographed it and thrown it back into the water, worried it would be illegal to keep. It turns out there is a name for this type of twinning: parapagus dichephalus – two heads, side by side, eye to eye. Two separate beings, one shared body, one shared life.

9

Out of the Blue

The Majestic Tea Room is tucked into the corner of an antiques centre – a boxy blue and white building on the northern edge of the Forth estuary. I'm here to meet Carol. After I saw the whalers that afternoon, I stood on Granton shore, ready to end my search for Anthony and cast the whaler's badge into the sea. But my hand had stopped; it felt like his story had not quite ended.

Soon after, I received a message via the genealogy account I had used to map Anthony's family tree.

Carol Ford had moved back to Edinburgh from the south of England. After visiting her great-grandfather's grave in Portobello, she began researching her family tree.

I just had a compelling urge to find out more, she wrote, *and I came across the family tree you're working on. How are you related?* she asked.

I wasn't, I said, but I told her I was researching whaling and had come across Anthony's grave in South Georgia. *Do you know anything about him?* I ventured.

No, I think he died young, before I was born. He would have been my uncle. My father was his brother.

I unravelled the story a little and sent her some links to explore, including one for Nicolson's documentary. I didn't want to be the one to tell her. By the time we arranged to meet, she knew everything I did.

The antiques centre, once a theatre, has long rooms thick with the smell of old furniture and the discarded bric-a-brac of life, mostly from house clearances – stuff the children didn't want or need once their parents had moved on: tired sofas, sideboards, coffee tables, bookshelves, umbrella stands, crockery, ornaments, fob-watches, clay bottles, avocado dishes and war medals at £10 a piece. A row of Davy lamps – miners' lamps – sits polished up on a shelf, testament to Fife's industrial past, before call centres and the Amazon depot.

After arriving early to explore the upper floors, I make my way back down the stone steps, worn by years of scuff up and down their tread. Standing near the entrance, a petite woman around my age, in a navy jacket trimmed with gold, turns as I walk past.

'Hello, I'm Carol.' She extends her hand to me.

I bypass her hand and pull her in for a hug; I feel relieved to find someone who cares about Anthony, someone I can pass him on to.

We take a seat at a melamine-topped table in the café and order hot drinks.

'It's hard to believe,' she begins. 'I've gone from knowing nothing about my family history to all this in the space of three weeks. I'm a little overwhelmed, if I'm honest.' Carol's face is framed by her neat hair, and I find myself wondering if there is any trace of Anthony in her blue eyes and pale freckled skin.

'When they said his name on that documentary, it made him feel so real, not just some distant relative on a family tree.'

'Did you know much about him?' I ask. 'Did your family ever talk about him?'

'Not really. I did hear something once about some kind of whaling accident. I remember I had a whale's tooth when I was young, though I don't know what happened to it. Maybe it came from Anthony. And I'd heard a rumour that one of my dad's brothers had taken his own life, but I didn't make the connection. I feel so sad about it, even though it all happened long ago. When I think of him out there, so young, no family, and probably no one to ask for help, it's . . . it's heart-breaking, really.'

Carol's tea arrives in a pot, a bone-china cup and saucer with yellow roses on the side set down beside it. I have one at home the same, wrapped in newspaper, tucked away in a drawer. It was my granny's favourite.

'What about the rest of the family, the other brothers?' I ask. 'They all seemed to have lived in lots of different places.'

'Well, Gerry, Anthony's younger brother, he'd been a whaler too – after Anthony. Perhaps he wanted to see for himself. Later in life, he emigrated to the US. My grand-mother Josephine moved there first with her daughter Mary, to work. She was quite some woman. She came back every year to see the family, but the boys all followed her event-ually. She did like her boys around her. Handsome they were too, by all accounts.'

Carol tells me that when she was young her own father Robert left to join his mother and brother in Chicago. Carol's mum had refused to go.

'Thank goodness she did. It's almost like that side of the family lived under a curse.' Gerry had two sons and called them Gerald and Anthony too. Both died in unrelated accidents in their late teens. A few years after he lost them, he took his own life. Aged fifty-two.

It seems unbelievable. Two sets of brothers, the same names, two generations: four tragic deaths.

'But I don't really remember them talking about Anthony,' Carol says. 'My granny was Catholic, so she must have told us to mind him in our prayers, but I'm only just learning the truth of it all now. I wonder why.'

I tell Carol the story of my friend Jamie. His family were Catholic too. 'It's changed now, but back then they didn't understand the impact of mental illness. When Jamie died, the local priest wouldn't allow him to be put in the village cemetery. Arrangements were made on the quiet with a priest from a neighbouring village instead.' I still feel a flush of anger talking about it. 'My mum took me to his grave once. Jamie's mother would never tell her where it was, but my mum found it. She would visit and lay flowers sometimes.'

In Spain, the dead are concreted into stacked slots in the cemetery walls; soil is too precious for burials. Jamie's grave was sealed by a slab of pure white marble etched with angels in delicate pale blue lines. It was beautiful.

'But there was no name, no date, no inscription at all. It all felt very much swept under the carpet.' I pause. 'The same might have been true of Anthony. They didn't understand depression. Perhaps it was all too hard to talk about.'

Carol's eyes tear up, and her pink fingernails lock around her teacup. 'It's so sad. I just think of poor Anthony out there on his own, no support at all. There should have been a duty of care. Why did they leave him behind?' Sad, then angry, then bargaining – 'If only he'd caught the boat home, he might still be with us today' – three of the five stages of grief in one breath.

'I can't help thinking how awful it must have been for my grandparents to get that news. Of course, we'll never know what the future might have held for him. But he's back in his rightful place in my family now. He won't be forgotten again.'

'Have you spoken about him to the rest of your family?'

'Yes, I've told them. It's funny how they've all reacted differently. It happened so long ago. I already know what I'm going to do, though.' Carol tells me that when she visited her great-grandfather's grave a few weeks ago in Edinburgh, there was room left on the headstone. 'I'm going to get a plaque made up for Anthony and have it put on there, in memory of him. I've already spoken to the cemetery manager about it.'

It's my eyes that well up now. 'That's the most perfect thing to do,' I say. 'It's like you'll be bringing him home.'

Carol nods.

'Oh, I have this for you.' I rummage in my bag for the Salvesen Ex-Whalers Club badge and hand it over to Carol. 'It belongs to you, really. Perhaps Anthony might have been one of those men in the club. He'd have had one of these.'

She holds it in the fingertips of both hands to look at it. 'I'd love to meet them – the friends he grew up with in Granton. They might have some happier stories about him. Can I contact them?'

I tell her that I'll put them in touch. Carol purses her lips and nods, still looking down at the small badge. We finish our chat and I offer her a lift to the station.

'No, thanks. I think I'll walk. I've a lot to think about.'

A few weeks later, Carol emails me a photo of Anthony. *Wow! Mary's son sent me this. It's the only one they have of him though the quality isn't great.* Mary was Anthony's older sister, no longer living, but she had remembered him, kept his photo all these years and passed it down to her son. I open the attachment.

It's a photo of Anthony sitting on a sea wall, about to jump off. He grins, great dimples in his cheeks and gangly arms too long for his sleeves, wearing a smart shirt and a zip-up cardigan. He looks well kempt, his hair short, though a few wayward curls have defied taming with Brylcreem.

I compare it to a copy of the photo from the archive, the one that made me think of Anthony: the young lad as he stands and watches in horror as a whaler hauls open the mouth of the baby whale on the factory deck. There is something familiar in the whaler's long slender arms, limp at his sides. The way he holds his hands. The sticky-out ears look similar, and the hair forcing its way out from under the cap. The lad in the photo looks much older, but these two photos would be years apart. I send it to Carol.

I don't think it's him, she replies. *It's just wishful thinking.*

I look again at the photos. She is right. The ears don't jut out quite as much, and the nose looks a little different. The hands look similar, but there is too much of an age difference. Her words catch me, though: *wishful thinking.* I wouldn't have wished that look of horror on Anthony. I wouldn't wish on him those sunken eyes or that sag in his shoulders. I am chilled by the feeling that this is what years of relentless whaling could have done to him. But it is not Anthony; it is some other lad who was once a bright young boy.

I arrange a call with Carol and her brother Martin. They have new information from the coroner's report into Anthony's death. I don't have access to it, but, as a family member, Carol was able to request a copy. The world is newly locked down in the midst of the 2020 pandemic, so the three of us arrange a video call.

'What I want to know,' Martin begins, 'is what the catalyst for his death was. At the moment I've got two, possibly three, different versions. None of it is clear, and it's all too easy to write off someone's life when it happened so long ago. But there had to be a catalyst, something that drove him to it.'

'It's certainly very muddled, and none of it quite makes sense,' I say.

'What is certain, though,' Martin continues, 'is that he did miss his boat home, probably because he was drinking the evening before, and he was stuck there for the winter.'

'And we know conditions at Leith Harbour were bleak,' I say. 'Being there for another year was not a good prospect, and young people have a very different sense of time too. At that age, a year would seem like forever.'

I remember John MacLean, the man I sat with at the whalers' lunch, telling me how he stood on the dock at Leith Harbour in the duffel coat his mum bought him, feeling the visceral pain of homesickness and how he just wanted to go home and couldn't. Homesickness is very real, often manifesting as depression, anxiety and withdrawal.

'But there must have been something,' Martin says, 'something that pushed him to do it.'

'I think that's the thing we'll never know,' I say. 'It was nearly seventy years ago, but even with people I've known who have taken their own lives, nobody's ever really sure what pushed them over the edge. It probably wasn't even a single thing.'

We know the brutality of whaling was traumatic for some like Ian, who told me his story at the whalers' lunch.

Slaughterhouse workers today exhibit high levels of trauma and post-traumatic stress, especially when coupled with poor and dangerous working conditions, high physical demands and extended working hours. On the *Southern Soldier*, Anthony was right on the front line of killing, and the work was relentless.

All of it adds up to enough – more than enough. We know how depressed he became: the withdrawal, the negative thinking, the idea that nobody liked him, that he felt useless. I've seen it all with G; they are classic symptoms of depression. 'He was a quiet lad, but turned even quieter around New Year,' one man said of Anthony. He'd been suffering for some time. But he is not to blame. He wasn't the first whaler to take his own life nor the last: bigger and tougher men than him stepped over the side of those factory ships, or walked out into the South Georgia winter, or worse, threw themselves onto their own flensing knives. The accounts from the time are all too brutal.

We'll never know the whole truth. We can only imagine.

Outlook

I walk up the hills behind our house on an October morning. Bickering geese trail their coffee-grind ribbons through the pale sky. Our north is turning away from the sun once more, and I feel glad to be back in the snug of my jacket; I still prefer the cold months. Last winter, the snow fell thick and lingered through the spring, sculpted by wind around the braille of the land, smothering the block-solid ground. The muffled world deterred all but a few hardy souls from making it this far into the hills.

Walking releases the stiffness from hours spent at my desk, many sat staring out the window as north winds race in to shiver the tops of larches. Next month's full moon marks five years since we set out for the Antarctic. This last year has unwound around me as I've sat in imposed stillness, writing my way through our journey, memories gifted back to me: the salt-spray and storms, rough hemp ropes, penguins in lucent seas, icebergs groaning like old men, and the rolling fin whales, their breath rising in pale morning light.

And you too, as I followed your journey south and dropped an ear into your short life: the bitter cold and graft of it.

It's quite a journey you took me on, Anthony Commiskey Ford. A look into a past I knew nothing of, and new, unexpected friendships. The whalers often send me photos they've turned out from battered boxes and drawers: them as brawny lads, and the ships they crewed. News arrives all too often of the loss of yet another of their members. At a time when the world seems ever more polarised, we are still joined by our shared humanity, by our grief and loss.

As I follow the path to the top of the hill, a walker rounds the corner ahead, and I step aside to give him a wide berth. It's been eighteen months since Scotland first went into lockdown: two whaling seasons and an overwinter since the pandemic reached our shores. We are over the worst, they say, but still, we tiptoe cautiously back to our daily lives.

I've needed this time of stillness to make sense of my journey south. For decades we've taken easy travel for granted; from cold climes to blistering tarmacs, little has been off limits. Yet what is the point of travel if we don't take the time to make sense of it? Antarctica was not the pristine wilderness I'd expected – of course not, otherwise I'd not have been there myself. And neither was it a great white empty space on which to write – or rewrite – our own stories. It is a complex, layered and nuanced place, defying simplistic tropes and narratives. It's a hard-edged continent with dashed-line boundaries, and humans have butted up against its uncertain borders for as long as they have suspected them to exist: exploring, conquering, exploiting, studying, occupying, claiming, naming, protecting and disputing. Many men, like Shackleton, were made famous by pitching themselves against its potency, but more were made wealthy plundering its abundance – mostly from a distance.

I crest the hill and walk to my favourite bench overlooking the Forth. Its silver thread glints from a gauzy landscape and runs east, releasing ships and ebbing tides into the North Sea. My mind follows them all the way to the Southern Ocean. I think back to those early explorers: Captain Cook as he fumbled his way south, then Carl Anton Larsen who built the first whaling station on South Georgia, paving the way for factory ships with their rear slipways, plan decks and exploding harpoons arriving en masse to cull whales: blues, fins, sperms, humpbacks, seis, minkes and southern rights.

I wonder at our fascination with whales, whether manifest as an Ahab-like obsession to vanquish, a search for serenity in their songs, a recognition of our solitude in the high-pitched echoes of 52 Blue, or the fierce need to risk life to protect them. They bring out the best and worst of us. Perhaps it is their quiet dominion over a part of the world we understand so superficially. Or perhaps it is the way they look at us. In moments of fear, animals often look away, as if that will stop the terror. But whales, it seems, don't look away. In their worst moments of pain and death, they will look right at you, eye to eye. If you happen to be there to see it.

In 2018, Japan finally withdrew from Antarctic whaling under growing international pressure and the continued campaigns of Sea Shepherd: 114 years after the first whaling station was set up on South Georgia, 110 years after mild-mannered Sidney Harmer first voiced his fears for the whale populations of the Southern Ocean, over 2 million dead whales later. Science, politics, negotiation and diplomacy are important but slow tools. Though Sea Shepherd's tactics are extreme and often risk the lives of the crew, in the absence of anyone able to enforce international environmental law, they were alone in taking radical and direct action to oppose the final years of Antarctic whaling. Paul Watson is unapologetic: 'Our society asks young people to risk their lives, to give their lives and to take lives all the time, to protect oil wells, real estate, flags and religion. I think it's a far more noble thing to risk life to protect endangered species or a threatened habitat.' It was needed. And it worked. The publicity generated worldwide shamed Japan into leaving Antarctic waters, though it still kills whales off its own shores, as do Norway and the Faroe Islands.

As I sit up on the ridge, my phone pings: an alert from our *Europa* group chat. We are all still in touch and have already had one reunion in London and another in Amsterdam. I made it along to the London one. Kate, Peter and Heikki were there too, and we met at the Maritime Museum in Greenwich to see an exhibition of artefacts from Franklin's expedition to the Northwest Passage. In the evening, we dined next to the Thames and drank into the early hours of the morning, loud and boisterous. I have a feeling that, like the whalers, we'll still be gathering and meeting up well into our old age.

Caught by the pandemic in Ushuaia in March 2020, and unable to continue her sailing season, the *Europa* crew hoisted her sails and turned her bow towards the Netherlands. She sailed across the Atlantic for eighty-two days without motor and without stopping. As we sat in our quarantine, we all followed her epic journey north through storms and doldrums until her eventual arrival in Scheveningen on 16 June 2020. Everyone in the *Europa* family who could be there to welcome her was on the dock, while thousands more of us tuned in online. It gave us all hope.

Heikki has posted a link on our group chat: an article from the British Antarctic Survey. The whales are returning to South Georgia! BAS has been surveying the seas around the island for many years. Up until 2018, only a single blue whale was sighted in twenty years. But in 2020, fifty-eight individuals were identified, and numerous more heard through acoustic monitoring. They've seen an abundance of humpbacks too, now estimated to be at ninety-two per cent of pre-whaling numbers. At a time when species are vanishing daily and the world feels bleak, these good-news stories are the precious gems we need.

South Georgia has also been declared rat-free for the first time in centuries. The South Georgia Heritage Trust, along with their American sister charity, the Friends of South Georgia Island, raised £10 million through private donations – including from the Salvesen Ex-Whalers Club – for the largest successful rodent-eradication programme in the world. Over three seasons, they used helicopters to drop 300 tons of rodent bait into every nook and cranny of the island. In 2017 and 2018, surveyors searched the island using rat-sniffer dogs. Not a single rat could be found. The most threatened ground-nesting birds are already thriving: pintails, Antarctic prions and the Wilson's storm petrels are all doing well, and the South Georgia pipit has returned from the brink of extinction.

The South Georgia Heritage Trust also partnered with the RSPB and BirdLife International to tackle the risk from fishing faced by albatross breeding on the island. Despite reduced bycatch in the waters around South Georgia in the early 2000s, nearly all the species breeding on the islands continued to decline. Albatross are global creatures, so the new partnership, the Albatross Task Force, tackled the issue on a global level. Simple and effective mitigations – fast sinking lines, bird-scaring streamers attached to long-lines and a switch to fishing at night – have reduced albatross deaths by ninety-nine per cent around the coastlines of South Africa. The project is ongoing, focused now on the fishing fleets off the shores of South America. Albatross breed slowly, so it will be some time before we know if the populations will recover, but it looks hopeful.

These are all important but tiny victories against the backdrop of unrelenting planetary exploitation. In March 2021, Netflix released their documentary, *Seaspiracy*, which exposed the global fishing industry, labelling it the greatest threat to marine life. Many attempts have been made to undermine and debunk the science behind the documentary, but it withstands scrutiny. The numbers are staggering: 300,000 dolphins, whales and porpoises are killed each year as bycatch; between 63 and 273 million sharks are killed every year; as much as seventy per cent of marine macro-plastic pollution is now made up of lost fishing gear; 24,000 fisheries workers are killed each year, with widespread forced labour reported in the industry; and, under current management, eighty-eight per cent of fish stocks will be below sustainable levels by 2050. Were he living today, mild-mannered whale advocate Sydney Harmer would undoubtedly be writing strongly worded letters to the government.

Though perhaps by now, Sydney Harmer would have been driven to more radical action, like the scientists today joining civil-disobedience protests around the world in their droves, clamouring for governments to act on the climate emergency. Some are on hunger strike, some daub our financial institutions with paint or break their windows, others glue themselves to motorways. Scientists have been sounding the alarm on climate change for decades while governments and the fossil-fuel industries have worked hard to sow doubt, divert attention, drown out or outright dismiss the stark facts. Just like the whaling companies did. Until it was too late.

We stand at a pivotal point in history, with two paths to choose. We can career along our tarmacadamed route to climate chaos and extinction, snuffing out the nourishing diversity of our planet and the life in our oceans, or we could turn our backs on the narrative of consumerism and unsustainable growth, stand against wealth extraction and hoarding, against the polluted cities and monocultured countrysides of this frenetic and unhappy Anthropocene life we have built. We might instead choose to tip our epoch into the Ecocene, to slow down and perhaps, like Bhutan, measure our success in happiness. And choose, like Shackleton, to leave no one behind.

It's not quite too late.

A skylark shoots up from the grass and explodes into song. The sun breaks through the clouds. As I turn to face its warmth, I look out towards Leith and am reminded of you.

A few weeks ago, Carol Ford wrote to tell me about the plaque she wants to put on the family's memorial stone in Edinburgh for you. The stone needs to be resited before they can attach the plaque, and the cost will be over £1,000. At my suggestion, Carol wrote to Alastair Salvesen to find out if they had a trust fund for the families of whalers killed in service to help bring the memory of you home. The billionaire replied that there was no such fund but referred her back to the men of the Salvesen Ex-Whalers Club.

My journey with you, Anthony, has come to an end. You have been seen. And you are remembered. When I think of you now, it's no longer the image of your grave back on South Georgia that stands out for me – or your final desperate act. In the same way, when I think of the two-headed whale, it's not the poor creature, ripped from the womb and splayed out on the flensing plan, that I see. I imagine instead a glorious full-grown two-headed fin whale, vast and black-backed, mottled under deep blue seas, surrounded by bright icebergs and growlers, lunging in double gulps of pink krill, its flanks propeller-scarred like spiralled Polynesian tattoos, an etched history of its long-lived lives.

The last year and a half has been especially hard on G. He'd been making good progress with his new therapist, had started visiting friends again, but with no distraction from his anxiety, and, indeed, a global pandemic to exacerbate it, he slept much of his time away, and his personal mire deepened. Though now there is a little light: there are days when he gets up and resumes his search of the horizon. On the wall, where we see it daily, hangs the painting of Point Wild. 'You understand,' he said when I gave it to him.

I manage to resist the undertow of his sadness now; his crippling anxiety makes sense to me in the face of relentless bad news fed to us on a daily basis. At what point is anxiety and depression not an illness but an appropriate response to the world? Yet my need to stay afloat is clear. My job is to stand in the life-raft and hold out my hand.

As I head back down the hill, I am paused by birdsong. Our home nestles in the hills, land reclaimed from sheep that displaced the communities who once lived here and left their mark in the crumbling stone walls and field boundaries now subdued to a light embossing of the land. The area is part of an ambitious habitat restoration plan by the Woodland Trust to turn 850 acres of barren grazing into native woodland, rich in mosses and frog-spawned hollows. Not long after I returned from Antarctica, I first noticed the birdsong: blackbirds and robins, finches, siskins, skylarks, wrens, thrushes and wood-peckers. For years, the skies here were mostly empty except for the winter caw of crows. This new habitat draws in such abundance; it is just one of the bright faces of tackling climate change.

I've loved having this time of slow travel to explore the richness on my doorstep. My world has opened up on a different scale, one that feels both intimate and expansive. The westerly winds sometimes bring me a whiff of the sea or fetch in squalls of summer rain, and on cold bright days the haar slips in from the east to lap at the foot of our hills. This land breathes to a slow seasonal rhythm and finally I am content to live in its gentle cadence. These are extraordinary times, we are told, yet war and plagues have festered since humans first walked the Earth. Civilisations come and go, life ebbs and flows. Our time will be marked in the thinnest layers of rock.

There are still moments when I feel my anxiety grow, for this planet and all we do to it, though I sense an untethering too, a letting-go of what I can't control. When the sadness and loss in me deepens, I close my eyes, put a hand to my belly and feel, secret in my breath, the long slow swell of the wild Southern Ocean.

The rise and fall of it.

Notes and Sources

The story of my trip to Antarctica on *Europa* in 2016 is based on the diaries I kept throughout the voyage and also on the incredible book put together by Jordi Plana Morales and the *Europa* crew. For the purposes of privacy, brevity and story-telling, I have changed the names of, and spliced together, my fellow guest travellers, though the permanent crew are all real. Places and events are real and conversations are as I remember them. Facts, figures and statistics were all rechecked at the time of editing and the sources listed under the chapter numbers below. Any factual errors or mistakes are entirely my own.

The life story of Anthony Ford as told in *The Two-headed Whale* is reconstructed from a scaffold of scant facts wrapped in stories from contemporary sources and the memories of men who were whaling at the same time as Anthony. Indeed, many knew and worked alongside him.

In terms of the facts, census and genealogy research provided Anthony's birth date and place, as well as the birth and death dates of his extended family and where they lived and moved to throughout their lifetimes. The Ford family, in particular Carol Ford, was able to fill in details

227

of Anthony's parents and to provide the background to Anthony's life.

Anthony's grave, on the island of South Georgia in the main Leith Harbour Cemetery, is listed on the South Georgia's Cemeteries website. The photograph there shows that the plaque on Anthony's gravestone incorrectly records his age as nineteen; he was only eighteen when he died. His first name is misspelled on the plaque.

The date and circumstances of Anthony Ford's death are recorded in the Register of Deaths on the above website. The coroner's report is held at the Scott Polar Research Institute at the University of Cambridge. While the report is embargoed until 2027, I inferred some of the circumstances surrounding Anthony's death from the MSc thesis *The Medical History of South Georgia*, 2008, by Dr Jennifer Keys, which can be downloaded from the South Georgia's Cemeteries website (see 'Further Information').

Rachel Hosker (Archives Manager and Deputy Head of Special Collections, Centre for Research Collections, University of Edinburgh Main Library) searched the limited crew lists held in the Salvesen archive. A Ford was listed as a deck/mess boy on the *Southern Venturer* in seasons 1949–50 and 1951–52. No crew lists for the other Salvesen factory ship, *Southern Harvester,* survive. If Anthony Ford was whaling for the seasons 1948–49 and 1950–51 as indicted in other sources, he likely sailed south on the *Southern Harvester* for these seasons.

The whaling stories and accounts were derived from a number of sources, including R.B. Robertson, *Of Whales and Men*, published by Alfred A. Knopf in 1954 (first edition). Publishers of subsequent editions included Macmillan & Co. in 1956 and Pan Books in 1961.

Robertson sailed as a physician on the 1950–51 Antarctic expedition with Salvesen. He does not mention the name of the ship that he sailed on, though he reports refuelling at Aruba – the usual stopover port for the *Southern Harvester*.

In *The Two-headed Whale*, I have taken Robertson's account of his whaling expedition as largely factual. Indeed, in his introduction to the book, he states that while the characters have been constructed from combining the traits of many of the whale men he met, he also endeavoured to give as true an account of a whaling expedition as he could. Cross-referencing and my discussions with whalers still living who are familiar with Robertson's book confirm that it represents an accurate portrayal of the Salvesen whaling expeditions of this time. Other descriptions of the conditions at Leith Harbour whaling station on South Georgia are close to that reported by Robertson.

John Burton's book, *Ta-ra, Johnny Boy: Boy Whaler to Rainbow Warrior*, published by FeedARead in 2021, gives a compelling account of his experiences of sailing with Salvesen. John's whaling career on the *Southern Venturer* spanned the years 1949 to 1952. John has a way with words, and his story, filled with details of day-to-day life at deck level, gives a different perspective to those, like Robertson, writing from a more privileged position. Though he thought nothing of it at the time, now in his eighties, John carries a heavy burden of guilt from his whaling years. His memory is scalpel-sharp, and he told me the good and bad of it. Sometimes, his voice cracked a little under the weight of his memories. The story of fixing the punctured hull of a catcher boat is one of his. John remembers the report of Anthony's death as he sailed back in to Liverpool at the end of the 1952 season.

The men of the Salvesen Ex-Whalers Club have been extraordinarily patient and generous with their time in answering my questions and telling me their stories. Jimmy Yorkston kindly welcomed me into their fold, and his brother Tommy Yorkston filled in some of the gaps in Anthony's young life and school days. Danny Morrison regularly took my phone calls and returned them in order to add more fascinating snippets of detail. Ian Moffat's story of looking the blue whale in the eye before she was killed provided valuable insight into the real trauma that could be experienced by these young men so far from home, as did John MacLean's story of the physical pain of homesickness that he suffered. These rare insights made imagining Anthony's life possible.

The Citadel Arts Group's booklet, *Whaling Days: Memories of the Leith Whaling Industry*, published in 2018, is a fascinating collection of stories from the whalers and their families. Many found their place in *The Two-headed Whale*.

Gibbie Fraser spent a considerable amount of time collecting and recording the memories from Shetland's whalers in *Shetland's Whalers Remember*, which he published in 2001. It was an invaluable resource for the writing of this book. The sinking of the catcher boat *Simbra* as told by John Leask was sourced from this volume.

Letters from a crew member written throughout the 1949–50 whaling season on the *Southern Venturer* are held in the archives at the Centre for Research Collections, University of Edinburgh Main Library. These provided many specific details in terms of the journey, the food and conditions on board the *Southern Venturer*. The stories of the gunners' strike, the stowaways boarding in Tenerife, the equator concert and the on-board pigs were all from the writer of these letters.

Other contemporary and historical accounts of whaling and Antarctica used as sources include:

Bennet, A.G., *Whaling in the Antarctic*, William Blackwood & Sons, 1931

Bourgon, L., *The Twilight of Britain's Antarctic Whaling Industry*, MLitt dissertation, University of St Andrews, 2017

Brown, N., *Antarctic Housewife*, Hutchinson, 1971

Cockrill, W.R., *Antarctic Hazard*, Philosophical Library, 1957

Does, W. van der, *Storms, Ice and Whales: The Antarctic Adventures of a Dutch Artist on a Norwegian Whaler*, William B. Eerdmans Publishing Co., 2003

Elliot, G., *A Whaling Enterprise: Salvesen in the Antarctic*, Michael Russell, 1998

Hart, I.B., *Whaling in the Falkland Island Dependencies*, 1904–1931: *A History of Shore and Bay-based Whaling in the Antarctic*, Pequena, 2006

Hart, I.B., *Austral Enterprises*, Pequena, 2020

Henry, T.R., *The White Continent*, The Scientific Book Club, 1950

Lillie, H.R., *The Path Through Penguin City*, Ernest Benn Ltd, 1955

McLaughlin, W.R.D., *Call to the South: A Story of British Whaling in Antarctica*, George Harrap & Co., 1962

Salvesen, R., *Ship's Husband,* Memoir Club, 2003

Sanderson, I.T., *Follow the Whale*, Cassell, 1958

Stewart, P., *Antarctic Whaling*, Dog Ear Publishing, 2018

Vamplew, W., S*alvesen of Leith*, Scottish Academic Press, 1975

Websites and sources relating to Antarctica and research cited were accessed in May 2022 and include:

CHAPTER I

Alexander, C., *The Endurance: Shackleton's Legendary Antarctic Expedition*, Bloomsbury, 1999

Bark *Europa*: https://www.barkeuropa.com

Sea Shepherd's eleventh Antarctic whale defence campaign, Operation Nemesis: https://www.seashepherdglobal.org/our-campaigns/operation-nemesis-11th-antarctic-whale-defense

Wheeler, S., *Terra Incognita: Travels in Antarctica*, Vintage, 1997

CHAPTER 2

Gaia Foundation, 'Love the Oceans? Stop Illegal, Unreported and Unregulated Fishing': https://www.gaiafoundation.org/love-the-oceans-stop-illegal-unreported-and-unregulated-fishing

IUCN Red List of Threatened Species (albatross): https://www.iucnredlist.org/search?query=albatross

Maritime Herald, 'Death, Drugs, Illegal Fishing and Twin Boats in the Port of Montevideo', 20 November 2018: https://www.maritimeherald.com/2018/death-drugs-illegal-fishing-and-twin-boats-in-the-port-of-montevideo

Žydelis, R., 'Amassed Threats to Albatross Species', *Nature Sustainability*, 1, 2018, pp. 81–82

CHAPTER 3

Cressey, D., 'World's Whaling Slaughter Tallied at 3 Million', *Scientific American*, 12 March 2015: https://www.scientificamerican.com/article/world-s-whaling-slaughter-tallied-at-3-million

Freedman, L., *The Official History of the Falklands Campaign*, vol. I, Routledge, 2005

Gordon, J.E., Haynes, V.M., & Hubbard, A., 'Recent Glacier Changes and Climate Trends on South Georgia', *Global and Planetary Change*, 60(1–2), 2008, pp. 72–84: https://www.sciencedirect.com/science/article/abs/pii/S0921818107000173

MercoPress, 'World's Best Climbers Tackle Shackleton's South Georgia', 29 August 2001: https://en.mercopress.com/2001/08/29/world-s-best-climbers-tackle-shackleton-s-south-georgia-feat

Poncet, S. & Crosbie, K., *A Visitor's Guide to South Georgia,* WILDGuides, Princeton University Press, 2005

Rocha, R.C., Clapham, P.J. & Ivashchenko, Y.V., 'Emptying the Oceans: A Summary of Industrial Whaling Catches in the 20th Century', *Marine Fisheries Review*, 76(4), 2014, pp. 37–48

Shackleton, E., *South: The* Endurance *Expedition,* Signet, 1999

Watson, P., Rogers, W. & Amory, C., *Sea Shepherd: My Fight for Whales and Seals,* W.W. Norton & Co., 1982

CHAPTER 4

Bonner, W., 'Impact of Fur Seals on the Terrestrial Environment at South Georgia', *Antarctic Nutrient Cycles and Food Webs*, 1985, pp. 641–46

British Antarctic Survey, 'Signy Research Station': https://www.bas.ac.uk/polar-operations/sites-and-facilities/facility/signy

Dunn, M. et al., 'Population Size and Decadal Trends of Three Penguin Species Nesting at Signy Island, South Orkney Islands', *Public Library of Science ONE*, 11(10), 2016: https://doi.org/10.1371/journal.pone.0164025

Fossi, C. et al., 'Fin Whales and Microplastics: The Mediterranean Sea and the Sea of Cortez Scenarios', *Environmental Pollution*,

209(2), 2016, pp. 68–78: https://www.sciencedirect.com/science/article/abs/pii/S0269749115301822

Gerats, S.: https://sarahgerats.com

Kelly, A. et al., 'Microplastic Contamination in East Antarctic Sea Ice', *Marine Pollution Bulletin*, 154, 2020: https://www.sciencedirect.com/science/article/abs/pii/S0025326X20302484

Klein, E. et al., 'Impacts of Rising Sea Temperature on Krill Increase Risks for Predators in the Scotia Sea', *Public Library of Science ONE*, 13(1), 2018: https://doi.org/10.1371/journal.pone.0191011

Readfearn, G., 'Microplastics Found for First Time in Antarctic Ice Where Krill Source Food', *Guardian*, 22 April 2020: https://www.theguardian.com/world/2020/apr/22/microplastics-found-for-first-time-in-antarctic-ice-where-krill-source-food

Secretariat of the Antarctic Treaty, *The Antarctic Treaty*: https://www.ats.aq/e/antarctictreaty.html

Taylor, M., 'Decline in Krill Threatens Antarctic Wildlife, from Whales to Penguins', *Guardian*, 14 February 2018, https://www.theguardian.com/environment/2018/feb/14/decline-in-krill-threatens-antarctic-wildlife-from-whales-to-penguins

CHAPTER 5

Alfred Wegener Institute, Helmholtz Centre for Polar and Marine Research, 'Depths of the Weddell Sea Are Warming Five Times Faster than Elsewhere', *ScienceDaily*, 20 October 2020: https://www.sciencedaily.com/releases/2020/10/201020105530.htm

The Conversation, 'Scientists Still Don't Know How Far Melting in Antarctica Will Go or the Sea Level Rise It Will Unleash', 20 September 2021: https://theconversation.com/scientists-still-dont-know-how-far-melting-in-antarctica-will-go-or-the-sea-level-rise-it-will-unleash-166677

Garbe, J. et al., 'The Hysteresis of the Antarctic Ice Sheet', *Nature*, 585, 2020, pp. 538–44

Harvey, F., 'Melting Antarctic Ice Will Raise Sea Level by 2.5 Metres – Even if Paris Climate Goals Are Met, Study Finds', *Guardian*, 23 September 2020: https://www.theguardian.com/environment/2020/sep/23/melting-antarctic-ice-will-raise-sea-level-by-25-metres-even-if-paris-climate-goals-are-met-study-finds

Jamison, L., 'The Legend of the Loneliest Whale in the World', *Slate*, 27 August 2014: https://slate.com/technology/2014/08/52-blue-the-loneliest-whale-in-the-world.html

National Marine Fisheries Service, U.S. Department of Commerce's National Oceanic and Atmospheric Administration, *Final Recovery Plan for the Fin Whale* (Balaenoptera physalus), 2010: https://repository.library.noaa.gov/view/noaa/4952

Strass, V. et al., 'Multidecadal Warming and Density Loss in the Deep Weddell Sea, Antarctica', *Journal of Climate*, 33(22), 2020, pp. 9863–81: https://journals.ametsoc.org/view/journals/clim/33/22/jcliD200271.xml

Trumble, S. et al., 'Baleen Whale Cortisol Levels Reveal a Physiological Response to 20th Century Whaling', *Nature Communications*, 9, 4587, 2018: https://doi.org/10.1038/s41467-018-07044-w

Turner, J. et al., 'Recent Decrease of Summer Sea Ice in the Weddell Sea, Antarctica', *Geophysical Research Letters*, 47(11), 2020: https://doi.org/10.1029/2020GL087127

Watkins, W. et al., 'Twelve Years of Tracking 52-Hz Whale Calls from a Unique Source in the North Pacific, *Deep-Sea Research Part I: Oceanographic Research Papers*, 51(12), 2004, pp. 1889–1901: https://www.sciencedirect.com/science/article/pii/S0967063704001682

CHAPTER 6

Burnett, D., *The Sounding of the Whale: Science and Cetaceans in the Twentieth Century*, University of Chicago Press, 2011

Calman, W., 'Sidney Frederic Harmer. 1862–1950', *Obituary Notices of Fellows of the Royal Society*, 7(20), 1951, pp. 359–71: http://www.jstor.org/stable/769025

CHAPTER 7

Archibald, M., *Ancestors in the Arctic: A Photographic History of Dundee Whaling*, Black & White Publishing, 2013

Britain's Whale Hunters: The Untold Story, produced by Keo Films and Shadow Industries, 2014: https://www.bbc.co.uk/programmes/b046pbk9

Burnside, A., 'The Scottish Billionaires' Club and How They Made and Spend Their Money', *Daily Record*, 12 April 2017: https://www.dailyrecord.co.uk/scotland-now/scottish-billion-aires-club-how-made-10208084

Dalyell, T., 'Sir Gerald Elliot: Scottish Industrialist Who Helped Set Off the Falklands War with Argentine Scrap Deal', *Independent*, 22 February 2018: https://www.independent.co.uk/news/obituaries/gerald-elliot-scotland-falklands-war-start-christian-salvesen-argentina-scrap-deal-a8221171.html

Edinburgh Evening News, 'David Bowie's Ziggy Stardust "born in Edinburgh"', 12 January 2016: https://www.edinburghnews.scotsman.com/news/david-bowies-ziggy-stardust-born-edin-burgh-629653

Historic Environment Scotland, Trinity House: History: https://www.historicenvironment.scot/visit-a-place/places/trinity-house/history

Macalister, T., 'Christian Salvesen Agrees to £254m Bid', *Guardian*, 3 October 2007: https://www.theguardian.com/business/2007/oct/03/3

McCurry, J., 'Japan Whaling Fleet Accused of Using Tsunami Disaster Funds', *Guardian*, 7 December 2011: https://www.theguardian.com/world/2011/dec/07/japan-whaling-fleet-tsunami-earthquake-funds

Rose, D. et al., '250 Labels Used to Stigmatise People with Mental Illness', *BMC Health Services Research*, 7, 2007: https://doi.org/10.1186/1472-6963-7-97

Archives of Messrs. Christian Salvesen Ltd., Edinburgh University Library Special Collections, University of Edinburgh, Coll-36: https://archives.collections.ed.ac.uk/repositories/2/resources/252

University of Edinburgh, 'Salvesen Archive – 50 Years at Edinburgh University Library – 1969–2019': https://libraryblogs.is.ed.ac.uk/edinburghuniversityarchives/2019/05/08/salvesen-archive-50-years-at-edinburgh-university-library-1969-2019

CHAPTER 8

Case, M., 'A Study of the Incidence of Disease in a Whaling Expedition to the Antarctic Pelagic Whaling Grounds 1946–7', *Journal of Epidemiology & Community Health*, 2(1), 1948, pp. 1–17: https://jech.bmj.com/content/2/1/1

Kompanje, E., Camphuysen, K., & Leopold, M., 'The First Case of Conjoined Twin Harbour Porpoises *Phocoena phocoena* (Mammalia, Cetacea)', *Online Journal of the Natural History Museum Rotterdam*, 2017: https://edepot.wur.nl/417381

OUTLOOK

BirdLife International, The Albatross Task Force: Reducing Albatross Deaths by 99%: https://www.birdlife.org/projects/albatross-task-force

British Antarctic Survey, 'Blue Whales Return to Sub-Antarctic Island of South Georgia After Near Local Extinction', ScienceDaily, 19 November 2020: https://www.sciencedaily.com/releases/2020/11/201119103058.htm

Calderan, S. et al., 'South Georgia Blue Whales Five Decades After the End of Whaling', *Endangered Species Research*, 43, 2020, pp. 359–73

International Whaling Commission, Bycatch: https://iwc.int/bycatch

Laville, S., 'Dumped Fishing Gear Is Biggest Plastic Polluter in Ocean, Finds Report', *Guardian*, 6 November 2019: https://www.theguardian.com/environment/2019/nov/06/dumped-fishing-gear-is-biggest-plastic-polluter-in-ocean-finds-report

Petursdottir, G., Hannibalsson, O., & Turner, J., 'Safety at Sea as an Integral Part of Fisheries Management', FAO Fisheries Circular, 966: https://www.fao.org/3/x9656e/X9656E00.htm

Read, A., Drinker, P. & Northridge, S., 'Bycatch of Marine Mammals in U.S. and Global Fisheries', *Conservation Biology*, 20(1), 2006, pp. 163–69

RSPB, The Albatross Task Force: https://www.rspb.org.uk/our-work/policy-insight/england-westminster/oceans-and-coastal/the-albatross-task-force

Seaspiracy, Seaspiracy Facts: https://www.seaspiracy.org/facts

South Georgia Heritage Trust, A Global Initiative to Protect South Georgia's Albatross: http://www.sght.org/south-georgia-albatross

Worm, B., 'Averting a Global Fisheries Disaster', *Proceedings of the National Academy of Sciences of the United States of America*, 113(18), 2016, pp. 4895–97: https://www.pnas.org/doi/full/10.1073/pnas.1604008113

WWF, 'Bycatch Is the Biggest Killer of Whales', 20 October 2016: https://phys.org/news/2016-10-bycatch-biggest-killer-whales.html

Acknowledgements

As a first book, this feels very much like a team effort. My gratitude is owed in spades to my fellow MLitt students from the University of Stirling: Theresa Moerman Ib, Debbie Bayne, Tineke Hegeman Bryson, Alex Prong and Craig Aitchison. Their own writings have inspired and motivated me, and they freely gifted honest feedback and invaluable support throughout. An earlier draft of the first part of this book was supervised as my dissertation by Kathleen Jamie. I am grateful for her subtle and discerning guidance. Liam Murray Bell, Chris Powici and Kevin MacNeil have put together a superb MLitt Programme in Creative Writing at Stirling, and I am indebted to them for their wisdom and feedback. Linda Cracknell provided essential mentoring throughout the production of the final manuscript. Without Linda's thoughtful and insightful input, this would never have become the book I'd hoped it to be. Jenny Brown provided valuable editorial advice and publishing guidance. Moira Forsyth at Sandstone Press encouraged me thoughout. Sarah Ream did a superb and timely job of editing, and I am grateful for her patient and gentle guidance through the process. Thanks to Hugh

Andrew, Jamie Crawford and the team at Birlinn for publishing this book in the UK. Thank you to Jen Gauthier, Jennifer Croll, and everyone at Greystone for their work publishing this book in Canada and the United States.

Carol Ford, Anthony's niece, has been unwavering in her support. I am much indebted to Carol, along with her brother Martin, for allowing me to write so honestly about their family. James Yorkston, Tommy Yorkston, Danny Morrison and the men of the Salvesen Ex-Whalers Club welcomed me and told their astonishing stories, and I am grateful to Liz Hare of the Citadel Arts Group for putting me in touch with them and for her work in gathering the whalers' stories for their publication *Whaling Days*. Ex-whaler turned Greenpeace activist John Burton has been generous and whole-hearted with his time, support and feedback for this book. He is a very special person to whom I owe much gratitude – not least for giving me so much faith in humanity. The team of the Special Collections in the Centre for Research Collections at the University of Edinburgh Main Library, and in particular Rachel Hosker, provided valuable assistance during my delves into the Salvesen archives. Thanks to Sarah Lurcock of the South Georgia Heritage Trust for leads and information and to Professor Stephen Trumble at Baylor University, Texas, for his fascinating insights into the world of whale earwax.

I am grateful to Captain Klaas Gaastra and his kind and capable crew for the journey of a lifetime onboard the *Europa*. Guide Lex van Groningen provided valuable feedback on the accuracy of the final manuscript. My fellow traveller Bel Burn gave me much encouragement and support. Thank you to Sue Clutton, Peter Biermans, Monica Brough, Maaike Verdult, Saskia Hogervorst, Saco Heijboer, Brigitte

Lauth, Jürg Frey, Jasi Frey, Fran and Tony White, Bruce James and the rest of the voyage crew for their good company and adventures – I look forward to seeing many of you at our next reunion.

My late mother, Sylvia Winterbottom, would have been ridiculously proud to have seen this in print. I take comfort in the fact that her generosity allowed it to happen. My dear friend Linda Smith continues to provide a firm anchor of support along with a strong link to my mother's memory.

So much love and gratitude is owed to my family for allowing me to run away to sea, and to G in particular for supporting me in writing so openly and honestly about him. He is, and always has been, an important advocate for openness on mental health issues.

We stay afloat together.

DAVID SUZUKI INSTITUTE

THE DAVID SUZUKI INSTITUTE is a companion organization to the David Suzuki Foundation, with a focus on promoting and publishing on important environmental issues in partnership with Greystone Books.

We invite you to support the activities of the Institute. For more information please contact us at:

David Suzuki Institute
219 – 2211 West 4th Avenue
Vancouver, BC, Canada V6K 4S2
info@davidsuzukiinstitute.org
604-742-2899
www.davidsuzukiinstitute.org

Cheques can be made payable to the David Suzuki Institute.